inside cupid's psyche

by
Joel Doerfel

Some rights reserved. You may share or remix this work, provided you make responsible use of the common—that is, give credit where it's due and share alike.

© Copyleft 2015 Long Yes Press

Published in the United States by Long Yes Press, longyespress@gmail.com.

Library of Congress Cataloging-in-Publication Data

Inside Cupid's Psyche / by Joel Doerfel.

Includes an index of first lines.
ISBN: 9780615896694 (softcover : alk. paper)

1. Economic Awareness. In your revolutionary thinking, start with economics. 2. Global citizen participation. 3. Social change—Global citizen participation. I. Doerfel, Joel.

Inside Cupid's Psyche by Joel Doerfel is licensed under a Creative Commons Attribution-NonCommercial-ShareAlike 3.0 Unported License. For more information, please visit:
http://creativecommons.org/licenses/by-nc-sa/3.0/deed.en_US

table of contents

preface   i

i. cadillac ranch   1

lit	3
victim	6
inside cupid's psyche	8
price of sleep	12
manifesto of love	17
omnisexual	20
ode to a mango	25
invisible man	26
nightswimming	29
cadillac ranch	30
incarnation	31
sleep disorder	32
xmen	35
christmas spirit	40
donkey	42
army	43
narcissus	45
what do i mean?	47
being, barred	50
definition	52
rotflmao mentalese	53
starstruck	55
ode to truth	56
libidinal labels	58
punctuality for naked souls	59
pay attention	61
mood music	63
on wave, wormhole, & wind	65
i said everything	67
amid the chaos of routinely	68

table of contents

the cat	69
so dies eidos	70
the node not taken	71
bellagio	72
even though	73
friend	74
imaginary action figures	75
impromptu	76
it's all about you babe	77
name-brand candy	78
ode to my parents	79
omen	81
perfection	82
persuasion	83
politics of friendship	84
possession	85
presence	86
re: hi!	87
roxanne & mephistopheles	88
sex party	89
sunshine	91
the devil's warrior	92
the force	93
the only poetry	94
this is a poem	95
touch	96

ii. in & out — 97

a hidden word	98
abecedarius of compliments	99
dream	100
five red apples	101
heartbeats	102

table of contents

ode to an oyster	103
ode to bikinis and insecurities	104
sein zum tode	105
passionfruit	106
anthem	107
do	108
strum	109
liquid courage	110
on dice & victory	111
heartcry	112
as it goes	113
roses	114
specific ally	115
cyberjava	116
in & out	117
infinity	118
with bukowski's cooperation	119
americana	120
tact & subtext	121
drunk	122
surprise	123
zarathustra's serpent	124
let me submit	125
being been	126
workshop	127
eye contact	128

iii. venice beach experiment   129

dealer	130
dreamvibe	131
meditation	132
voyeurs & players	133
shepherds & midwives	134

table of contents

you	135
do you?	136
ride	137
letting go	138
flow	139
identity	140
what books assume	141
training day	142
anti-postmodernism	143
lullaby	144
delivery	145
heroes	146
on praise & blame	147
assembly	148
distinction	149
universal atheism	150
style	151
lovedrug	152
how to learn a name	153
love	154
amoeba	155
(overheard in the subtext)	156
houseguests	157
race (or how we learn)	158
counterpoint	159
ucla	160
…or	161
lovespell	162
everything nothing	163
leveling	164
venice beach experiment	165
context	166
pain	167
metamorphosis	168
a new math	169

table of contents

waterfront	170
intrusion	171
spectator sport	172
being & time	173
meditation	174
ode to my lover	175
observation	176
thisbe's eyelids	177
ode to an atheist with a god-complex	178
mindstretch	179
ask	180
what's with you?	181
on bukowski & hollywood	182
tao	183
ancient wisdom	184
on personal gods & household idols	185
portrait of a young woman as an artist	186
worlds apart	187
on families & self-resemblance	188
here	189
for vanessa	190
heartcry	191
...to the beat	192
two people, one evening	193
rhapsody on rilke	194
this is a good avocado	195
guide	196
for a.r.w. (a sonnet)	197
for you	198
eyes, hearts & tongues	199
metaphor	200
billy idol	201
fame	202
not black & white	203
autopoesis	204

table of contents

ode to anaxagoras & deleuze — 205
given — 206
playgrounds — 207
select company — 208

index of opening lines — 209

preface

Inside Cupid's Psyche was conceived during the turbulent, beautiful spring of 2004, in the small town of Amarillo, Texas. I'd been writing free verse and Shakespearean sonnets for several years when I accepted an entry-level teaching post at a nearby university. Kevin, one of my more *avant-garde* colleagues, learned of my love for poetry and invited me to a performance. I had to get in.

Immediately, I started performing poetry on the intimate, vibrant local circuit. So began my "slam phase," which developed meteorically for two years and continues to influence my art to this day. Back then, if you couldn't find me writing lines at Roaster's Café, I might well be performing with the likes of the late Kevin Krone and the late Hunter Ingalls (the pair to whom this work is dedicated), Alberto Herrera, Lesley Shelton, Superfly, or Elena Rodriguez. In Amarillo circa 2003, creative culture was something you either found and cherished or invented with like-minded artists. I thank my co-creators for their art.

Alongside the undeniable effects of an ethos of performance poetry and the inspiration of my fellow performers, my poetic influences from early in this era include Saul Williams, Eminem, Canibus, NAS, Nuyorican Poets Café, Bob Dylan, Neruda, Bly, Shakespeare, and Eliot. Floating to the top of my philosophical influencer list were Nietzsche (whose entire corpus I read during these years, with a keen eye for "On Truth and Lying in an Extramoral Sense" (1873)), Foucault (especially *History of Sexuality,* which heavily influences the poem "inside cupid's psyche"), Lakoff & Johnson (I still muse that language, and most of cognition, is metaphor all the way down), and Heidegger (look out for references to "Dasein.") Classical thinkers like Plato and Aristotle make their mark as well, since I read their corpus during this time. The influence of Deleuze emerges toward the end.

The poems from the early portion of this collection also reflect the "Storm and Stress" of a young man amid radical life change. Career-wise, they reflect my move from graduate school to a teaching position, and my studies for comprehensive exams—for which I became intimate with about 20,000 pages of philosophical classics from Thales to Derrida, over the course of about a year. I moved from Pittsburgh to Amarillo for the job, but also to escape increasingly stifling religious oppression aimed at a newly minted evangelical-turned-atheist. Imagine moving *to* Texas to escape religious dogma. I was in the process of being ostracized by many of my religious friends, solidifying my perspective that contemporary religious practice in America is primarily a social phenomenon (as it has been throughout our species' existence). Two years in Texas gave rise to 18 months in Los Angeles, after which my then-wife and then-I divorced in late 2005. Hard years followed, accompanied by the empty solace of voluminous cigarettes and beer, and a hiatus from Los Angeles. The convalescent's strength returned, and I rekindled my ongoing affair with the City of Angels in 2007.

There's always a silver lining, and from my first years in L.A. (2004-2005), as well as my current stay here (2007 to present), I've forged some beautiful and virtuous friendships, called Black Rock City home, and, along with increasingly frequent sparkling moments of joy and dancing, I've exercised copious amounts of self-overcoming. This collection ends with poems from 2008.

To paraphrase Aristotle, "Virtue is forged in struggle." My most trying years to date have led to a beautiful personal freedom, an unshakeable philosophical humanism, and a poetic style that reflects both. Thus, the early poems in this collection pulsate with a philosophically radicalized energy that matures into a more meditative tone toward the end. Throughout, each poem reflects a ruthlessly non-conformist, life-affirming creation of values.

As Nietzsche has it, "Noble morality...is rooted in a triumphant Yes said to oneself. It is self-affirmation, self-glorification of life, it also requires sublime symbols and practices, but only 'because its heart is too full.' All of beautiful, all of great art belongs here: the essence of both is gratitude" (1888, *The Case of Wagner*, "Epilogue").

These poems are a monument of gratitude to all who have been a part of my journey, great and small, friends and enemies, and everyone in between. I joyfully enjoin each and all with the Nietzschean rally: have the courage of your own-most sacred No to all forces that oppose your highest, longest will and let the forests of the world resound with the roar of your sacred Yes to Life!

— Los Angeles, 2015

i.

cadillac ranch

lit

lit
like a cigarette
whose smoke meanders
toward the sky,
& dances with the wind
whose body
looks back often
on its birth
in the earth
and its days
in the sunshine
as tobacco, harvested
as trees
made pulp
as synthetic filter
patented 78 years ago
by an organic chemist
everyone forgets.
all these factors
factoried,
then bought,
then lit,
now crackling,
burning,
slowly
& inexorably
toward its end,
only to end
in an ashtray
in a trashcan
in a landfill,
eroding,
becoming...

engaged
like the wheels
of a roller coaster
when the electricity
kicks in
and the ride
has begun
and the coal
has become
steam

that turns
turbines
and is sent
line after line
into the time
that the screaming children
waving their hands
in the heat
had on the ride
that's only just now beginning
and is already

committed
like the man
in the asylum
in the university
in the profession
that professes its truth
and proselytizes
its converts
so well
that the hell
they endure
and call "culture"
seems like
the isles of bliss
and all of its institutions
that did not arise
by decision
but by some random fuck
in the backseat of history
give us the genealogy
of our traditions
that we say
would not exist
unless people
and tribes
and corporations
got

married
like partners
playing a child's game
beneath a lattice-work
of vows
and indiscretions

and all of this
has been arranged
beforehand
and the only
choice
is the choice we make
day by day
to embrace the fate
that has coupled us
with this life
because
the only other option is

divorce
like a darkness
like exile
to a *terra incognita*
to a land where
enemies of the state
are sent and never return
whose distant sounds
we hear
in the silence of the night
of fires crackling
of children screaming
of earth in its churning
and the doubts
and the fears
are returning
because
how do i know
if i could ever
weather
such a night?
and i'm still afraid
of the dark.

victim

am i a victim? am i a slave?
am i a glow-stick in humanity's rave?
am i a savior or do i need to be saved?
am i an ink-blot on history's page?
am i a number,
a vote in a box
or a gear in a car?
or a wheel
or a star
misaligned?
rusty shocks,
broken struts,
running ruts in my life
through the habits you gave
while society's track-marks,
greased to the grave,
lie thin on my skin above veins
whose hemocytes crave
your ideologies.

does my dad or my preacher
tell me how to behave?
does the state mold my fate
& dictate my thoughts
about what i can claim as my rights?
private life, private liberty,
private property...
i'm confused—
who wrote the poem?
was it i or my muse?

who's to blame?

who's to blame
if my homework's not done
when i step into the classroom of reality?
& who's to blame
if i forgot to study
for the tests of history?
"it's just that i was so busy
& pressures came up
that i couldn't avoid...& i caved...."
& now i'm fucked up.
look what i did.

was it my ego?
or was it my id?

does it matter?

victors write history
on the backs of victims, wiped clean.
& the whining we hear
is the screech of the dominant chalk on the slate,
on the *tabula rasa* of lives,
on the *carte blanche* that every victim provides.

i'm always the page.
but i'm also the pen.
when the victim-mentality
whimpers & sighs with invisible ink,
it's especially then
that the fluids of victors
run virile & black.

just like you, sometimes too,
i fall flat on my back...
what i lack
is *excuses*.

what i did is what i did.
& i am the deed,
not the ego or id.
& what i *can* change
i *will* change,
because i *take* responsibility.
& i *learn* from mistakes.

do you want someone to blame?
blame me.
it's my fault.
& after i've served my time
in the vault,
i'll come by,
& you'll bend over for me
to write *my* history
on *your* back.

inside cupid's psyche

LIBERTY,
statue of.
statute-love
& statutory rape
of the intellect.
life liberty & property
where sex
is just a word
unheard in ancient greek
symposia where socrates
made passes at underage drunk boys;
where names like
faggot, pedophile, & pederast come
into the minds of classicists,
supersaturated with
masturbatory fantasies
of venus on a half-shell.
& who knows why
the penis of the past fell
into their hands erect
like the statue of liberty
blue-green lady
blue because she can't figure out
what liberation means
from lust
& gender wars
& libidinal economies
green by default envious
in the meantime
greed takes over:
  thou SHALT covet thy neighbor's wife...
  thou SHALT covet thy neighbor's ass...
covered with confusion like a blanket
blank stares
when you ask her WHY she likes it in the ass
but she's sure
because she's heard
that she only uses 10% of her ovaries
& that the inuits have 19 words for vagina
outdone only by the french
to whom we owe so much
for the kisses & the ticklers
& the sexual revolution,
because we now enjoy...

EQUALITY--

equal rites & rituals, regrets;
equal unemployment,
deployment,
girls-&-boys-bent-
over-backward
equally by the armies of the androgynous.

who used to chant
"men are for pleasure
& women are for making babies"
like a mantra
but their tantras
are private now;

nights rewind their
daytime pleasure-piles,
lightcone-piles
for a sexuality
that's the laughingstock
of fashion moguls
seven generations down the line.

feminism,
quickies, nooners,
condoms & diaphragms
once built our equality,
pleasure-based ecology,
obsolete monogamy,
& who said that survival was a drive?

probably some obscure,
deranged anti-postmodernist
raving about

FRATERNITY

& sorority
keggers that drown
maternal instincts
down
the sink-hole
toilet-bowl
of a paternal politics

whose friendship
lasts a lifetime
of one-night stands
at carnal carnivals.
car seats too small
to make out
the handwriting on the wall.

grand confusion
mental contusion
lacerated-lobe-
noise-lesions,
girl & boyhood reasons,
& ape-deployed legions
of personalized ringtones,
sling stones
shot at the inner ear
by the familiar
cellphone static phrase
"my place or yours?"
OR
"i saw your sister yesterday..."
OR
"didn't we meet at the
alpha-incest-omega party?"
(that time I was
sucking your tits, earlobe &
necromancing the stone-cold
stares of my sisterly admirers...)

& what I realized
when I saw freud fucking foucault
at the nudist colony
is that even oedipus needs an aphrodite,
like cupid needs a psyche
who never looks her urges in the face
so that he can perch
with invincible arrow-tips
dipped in
the unknown logic of the pheromone
atop the bastille of sexes
to ensure that the war will not be won,
& to keep humanity
happy, procreating, & brain-numb
numb to the fact that
humans make love.

humans make love.
blinding love, making
us invisible, forgotten selves
who treat sexuality
like a stone circle of miraculous origin,
like stones that fall from tongues,
marvelous meteors formed from
forgotten metaphors by minds,
angels & demons
& broken wet-dream fronts
in bed with
the unseen foes
of our own desires & drives...

increased heartbeats, boners & breasts
pound out the human marathon of
mutual masturbation,
(coincidentally procreation),
which comes as no surprise--
where only beholders have eyes--
& artificial hearts are
beating nature's compromise:

SEX IS NOT OVERRATED.
IT'S UNDERANALYZED.

price of sleep

what is the price of sleep?

& what can you exchange for purity?
or pay for contentment?
or trade for denial?
or barter for a little r & r?

$7.00 for a bottle of demerol?
or 4 for ny-quil liqui-caps,
elixir that's
a liberation from waking life,
libation that's taking life
4 hours at a time
sublime paradox of an *r-e-m* cycle
that circulates both *ram* & *rom*
only fry the circuits of your subconscious drives
with the river-water of forgetting.

& what is the price of sleep?

what is the price of keeping up your vain appearances
adherences to arbitrary etiquettes--
                                is it a hard day's work?
...but the price-tag of sleep is too high
when the cost is your life & your time
is too valuable
'cause you could be out-earning,
fulfilling your yearning
for power
the hour's too late. it's 4am
& your mother, the state,
dictates to your social-security number
that it's time to slumber
but you can't
'cause your sycophant,
somnambulating thoughts of what
your investments might do overnight
make you insomniac.

so you lie on your back,
when it's time to rest,
but you can't
uncertain of the future of the west,
afraid that the sun

of tomorrow's undone world-economy
might rise in the *east*.

& the cost of your sleep is a prayer
& a quest for the truth, for a god,
for the truth
that
god is resurrected
       god is undead
& that those who are made in his image,
are the born again
zombies & vampires
of capitalist descent
who save up for
frontal lobotomies
and / or teeth that have been filed down to
oil-sucking fangs.

whose mind is numb to what they've done
& what they're doing; who are
in the world
but *dead* to it,
doped on hope,

sleep-walkers,
day-walkers,
blind to the world
with eyes wide open
who live,
like their god,
in a land where there is no sleep,
no *night*,
no evil powers left to fight,
only absolute wrong & right
in a land… in a land… in a *land*
whose promise is that
god is america… & america is god
whose cash-crop
is the wheat & the tares
of the amber waves of grain,
manifest destiny that is still
claustrophobic on an open plain
& dissatisfied with sea to shining sea…
economic imperialism
of a nation whose alleged

foundation is christian principles,
& whose money still preaches, "in god we trust,"
as it goes overseas
to explode un-belief
& convert new militia
to its swarms of undead
with a bite on the neck
or a claw to the head
& soon everyone will see it your way
because
seeing is believing in the land of no eyelids.

so what is the price of sleep?

counting the ways in which you're a sheep,
a shallow consumer that grazes
relational greens,
a fickle follower
who goes with the flow
but forgot how to grow
into a leader, or a lover of humankind,
or a river of life that overflows,
since you just drink from
whatever giardia creeks
your meek & timid pasture-mates may find.

while the four stomachs of your mind
continue to ruminate
your narcissus & poppy blooms
whose opiums of hope
& crack-whore capitalisms
only raise your dopamine & serotonin levels
enough to join
the contagious yawn of humanity.

of course you can't sleep.
your haven't paid your social income tax!
15%, 30%,
30 shekels of silver that it costs for
a climaxed clitoris, or a semen-emptied cock,
correct alignment of the spine,
supine or prostrate
prostituted emptiness of mind.

the amount of the bribe
that continues to climb

for parole from your life-sentence
to the prison of care,
incarcerated there
for the nightly murder of
the fire-breathing furies,
the waking-life worries
that go by the names of where, when, & why…

but what were you supposed to do?
you needed to sleep…
to dream an escape,
to rest after the creation
of today's universe,
to live its cosmic history in a nod,
& churn out
a burning apocalypse
that would turn
your conscious universe into
the stardust of a dream.

you need to escape,
to be *out* like a *light*
but instead you're
in, like a *darkness,*
a mental malaise,
seeking a sleep
in which
your heartstrings are cut
from the villainous puppeteers
of desire & regret.

content to sleep like a corpse
since you can't sleep like a baby.

what is the price you pay for sleep?

how much you ate
& when you exercised?
life ruled by an hour-hand,
minute-hand,
second-hand morality
& second-helpings
of super-sized
mcdonalds value meals.

what is the price of sleep?

& what can you exchange for purity?
or pay for contentment?
or trade for denial?
or barter for a little r & r?

$7.00 for a bottle of demerol?

manifesto of love

shut the fuck up and listen--
my manifesto of love
will glisten in the morning
like the wings of doves,

will roll like the ocean
with its crashing waves,
crushing all your subcultures
that tell me how to behave.

my drift
will pulverize & sift
these cherished myths
and turn to shifting sand
the monotonous boulders of monogamy
and the boring decorum
that goes by the name
of "boyfriend" & "girlfriend"

my riptides rumble,
rush & crumble
the terrible cliffs of postmodernism
whose pillars disavow
that truth may be contained,
but post with unseen malice
the banns that put
my passion in a chalice.

i smash
these two new tablets
whose patrimonious verdicts put
truth on parole
but give love a life-sentence
on the death-row of matrimony.

i drown
these institution-codes
that would arrest my flood,
distill my salts
& evaporate enough of me
to pour
my whole love
pure
into a *cup*.

yes,
this
is my manifesto of love
my declaration of independence
from the games
that they play
that make love
fake.

my love is **true**
but not with
a truth that's
cookie-cut
from the dough
of american wet dreams

or stored up
in some platonic castle on a cloud
surrounded by ceremonial white pikes
on which impaled and smiling
sit
the decapitated heads
of my 2.3 kids.

no,
my love *is* my truth
woven into the fibers
of my organism,
this indiscriminate social animal
i've become.

& i tangle my antennae
with the *whole* world
because i know
i have enough love
to make the cosmos my companion
since everyone who touches me
becomes
infused, confused, & transfused
with my being.

and i embrace
the fact that
love, respect, friendship and sex
all share a syntax

because
my passion for life
is my passion for you
and my lust
is a lust
for what **you** will become

and if you hear what i'm saying
and you know
that your love
and your lust
and your truth
must also swell
beyond
the cages of cultural conformity,

then come *walk* with me
and let me share with you
the fierceness of my being;

and come *learn* from me
how this symbiosis with all things
gets lived in my corner of the world,

and come *join* me in my relentless quest
for a furious intimacy
with the world
and with you.

omnisexual

i am the first omnisexual,
the first antisexual.
so don't fucking put me in your little boxes
of "gay" or "straight" or "bi."

                                      i am a willing pervert,
                                      because in a world this fucked up,
                                      the only road to sanity
                                      is deviance.

which is why
i pose my question to the worldly wise:
how'd you get so obsessed with sex?
& who gave you your turn-ons
& the logic of your hard-ons?
society?
what you grew up with?
what you've tried?
men? women?
boyfriends? brides?
brunettes or redheads?
intellectuals? airheads?
toys? tantra? kinky sex? or 69?
if it's just a matter of taste,
then take from the buffet whatever fate puts on your plate
because
        vegetarians are just as criminal as queers.

& if you're not a social puppet,
but instead, you think your will is "free,"
your tastes are still arbitrary.
instead of social-chefs,
you're the one
who makes the choices
from the carnal smorgasbord.
you choose,
you will,
you judge,
you arbitrate.
at any rate,
your lusts are arbitrary.

for instance, gentlemen,
what's up with penetration?
        what's the obsession with

             "sticking it in" somewhere?
             why a vagina?
             an ass?
             a mouth?
             why not a sock?
             or a sofa?
             or a blowup doll?
             or a sheep?

come on,
it all feels the same
when you stick it in,
provided there's adequate lube.
             & everyone wants orgasms,
             because pleasure is our deepest ground & goal,
             even if the tall, dark edifices of ideology obstruct it.
             ...although every *she* can pleasure herself
             as well as any *he*...
             today's homos & heteros keep on seeking *we*.

girls, on the other hand,
want love.
at least,
so the story goes...
... though every social relation
has its emotional connection,
& you can be in love with me
without ever touching me
with a communion of minds
that is deeper than any
two bodies bumping & grinding...
                         since love does not
                    require sex.
& most of our libido is symbolic anyway:
erotica's a shadow-realm.
it's all a dream. it won't come (true).
& so
we men, erect.
we women, wet.
(who dream of sexing
night & day,
disappointed with the last climax
& imagining the next,
in love with what we think we want,
in love with reveries,
black sex-holes into which we hurl our mental energies.)

>   we fuck the air
>   & get off by dry-humping our dreams.
>   while the imaginary torsos
>   against which we heave & thrust
>   provide no friction
>   since they're just
>   the ghosts & shadows of our love,
>   frigid reflections of what we lack
>   symbols that fly through our heads
>   while we lie on our back,
>   forever fantasizing,
>   but never realizing
>   that the tail we've been chasing all this time
>   is our own.

pornographic fantasies,
feeling-fabrications,
shadowplays
sponsored by
narcissus-societies
in love with visions of
intangible, two-dimensional images
floating across
the big screen,
the small screen,
the inside screen,
the inside scene,
seen from behind the eyelids,
daydreams,
nightdreams,
wet dreams
become
the ghosts that motivate our appetites & unfulfilled designs,
reflections & projections on
the impenetrable wall
of our own inadequacies;
whose forms we fixate on so much
that we crave their impossible touch
more than life itself.

blind lust for the kind of omnipotence
that would substantialize
the gods & idols
of our minds.

& even if it were just in our minds,
our libido would be ubiquitous,

since it evaluates & clings to
our every thought.

but sex is not just in our minds.
it's in our being.
humans are sexual beings—
homo erectus, homo eroticus.
eating, sleeping,
having conversations,
living, loving—
everything we do is connected
to our being,
being-sexual....

& so i leave you to your ordinary sexualities,
your "gay" & "straight" & "bi,"
to a sexuality that is
either arbitrary or socially-determined,
that is
symbolic,
ubiquitous,
& driven by pleasure & "love."

but as for me, i will cherish my body
with its erections & its ejaculations
but i will not come into your boxes
(into your vaginas & your rectums
& your throats
& your farm animals;
into your cubicles
& your sons & your daughters
& your idealisms)
i will not come into your boxes...
...and i will!
and i will come into the world
and my semen will be everywhere
and it will be the air that you breathe
& the poem that you read
because
                        i have become my sexuality
for all & none of you
and / or
for all & none of me
unsexy, sexy, fated, free;
unsexed & sexed, while flexibly
i am becoming, sexually—

the first antisexual,
the first omnisexual.

ode to a mango

what do you mean to advertise,
mango,
with your rainbow of soft, freckled skin…
red, orange, yellow, green…
seducing me from the street corner?

does your dad, the tree, approve of this?
but it is your power to forget,
to make me forget—
your roots,
your cells patiently soaking up the orange sun
     day after day,
your childhood dangling against the blue sky,
the essence you collected
        moon after moon—
all that you've come here to spend.

you…i…forget the capitalist who sent
the starving old man with dark wrinkled skin
to pick you.

advertising ripe virginity in the cool shadows
you lure me, dare me to think
what's inside your soft, pink outer skins.
you tease me to pleasure your
wet, fibrous flesh with my mouth.

you promise—
chaste, fertile, shy—
to outstrip all other orgasms;
all my customary cycles.

i want to be eaten like a mango:
all my forgotten life-juices stored up
for one sweet, seductive moment;
devoured at once
by a hole in the earth.
part of her cycle
but breaking her routine,
making her shudder
with rare ecstasy.

invisible man

the brown mass
with its earthy aroma
passes through
the ass
and says "plop"
to porcelain
and water.

this conversation
takes place
behind closed doors.

and the hygiene
of two-ply toilet paper
hides
the transgression,

as if we were embarrassed about
our bodies
or had disowned them.

we want
so much
to be invisible.

we want to forget
that we as organisms need
to eat,
digest,
and shit.

we silently deny
with pads & tampons
that we as humans
bleed.

condoms,
catching semen,
cloak from memory
the mortal miracle
of pregnancy.

and anti-perspirant
and urinals

stand like monuments
that would erase our minds
of pheromones,
of the elixirs
of our natural attraction.

so we surround ourselves
with the props of our forgetting--
q-tips & clearasil,
shampoo, eyedrops,
toothpaste, & razors--
so that our pores
now ooze with different oils
as we wish away
our body follicles.

mascara, lipstick,
base & powder
fix us to face
the stage
of real life,
painted.

prozac & ibuprofen
shift & hide
the balance
of our moods.

costumes cover naked apes.

and leaving the sheltered artifice
of our apartments
we hop into cars
that take us distances
too far for legs.

we get to the high-rise,
take the elevator
to our floor,
and sit at
our computers,
our man-made brains.

or go to super-walmart
for groceries
and / or handguns

although we have
no need
to hunt or gather now....

we have forgotten our bodies.
although the shift was subtle & slow
like sandy sediment hardening into rock
or the drift of a few consonants or vowels,
that nonetheless change
hippocrates into hypocrite,
& faber into fabrica.

and though the ancient savage
was no more noble
than today's suits on wall street,
at least
he lived in his own skin
& wasn't ashamed of his body.

but now, somehow,
the body has become invisible.
with caked-on makeup, clothes & restroom doors
the facade is no longer translucent.
no sun will shine beneath this social shell.
in fact, we'll go from here
with our veneer
& all our nice, polite appearances.

but now,
just for a moment,
imagine
that you love your body.
love it when it poops & pees
and bleeds
and sweats
and cries
and gets zits.

& see yourself
in all your flesh,
in all of your fragile humanity.

& own the only skin
your organism has
to perform in.

nightswimming

karma lingers from the skating rink.
we skated like fools,
and had a drink,
and laughed
when my fingers got sticky with your pink
cotton candy.

it was hot
and muggy
and long ago.

and we went hiking
and you scraped your arm
on a rock.

so we headed home
and got you a bandage,
and went to sonic
for some slurpees.

and i don't know why it sticks with me
like this--

the sand volleyball,
and nightswimming;
starry skies on high school summer break,
before i knew what love was,
or worried about budgets.

what was it we shared
in those moments?

day and night
meant something different,
and remembering was a thing of the future--

THIS future,
in which i reminisce on our first kiss
and the duck pond
and the insecurity,
and you,
and me,
hopeful and exuberant.

cadillac ranch

you're lucky,
yellow town,
an eccentric artist
snuck in among your moguls
& populated your neighborhoods
with postmodern street signs.

you're lucky,
yellow town,
split down the middle by two counties,
one wet, one dry,
whispering, just like everything else,
"have y'all sold your soul to our social club?
well then y'all just earned our howdy smile."

you're lucky
your old money
from cattle & oil & land
recycles among newer ventures.

you're lucky
for the cliché sorority girls & the jazz
& the symphony & the beat poets
& the art & the locally-owned cafés.

otherwise,
almost no one would stop
on their way across country.
maybe to gorge on your huge steaks,
but that's about it.
they've heard your halfjoke warning
not to mess with your state, but

you're lucky
none of them will remember the alamo
the way they remember
those 10 late luxury models,
iron goliaths,
planted head-down
in the desert sand,
a flamboyant commune of
rainbow ostriches.

incarnation

you have seen me
in all of my humanity.
you have been with me
in all my scabs & scars,
in my sweat & heavy breathing,
in the smell of my feet,
in the halting poetry of my toes,
in the universe of my hands,
& the tickle of my hair,
in my laughter
& insecurity,
with my soul laid open
before you
like the juice of an orange
just-sliced.

and you have loved me.

you sip & savor
my existence,
my passion,
& my despair.

you lie with me
& embrace me
like the waves embrace the sand,
caressing me like the wind,
burning me with your fire,
drinking me with your roots:
without hesitation,
without regret,
you nourish me
and know me
as we become
one flesh.

sleep disorder

my paths of thought that run
through fields of memory
are lit by rays of hope
or overcast by shades of doubt
& specters of my discontent

my sleep is a goddess who will not be wooed.
a sandman whose hands have stopped taking my bribes
& a body of secret laborers
that laugh like
powerful proletarians poised to overthrow
the power-politics of my realm of rest.

my insomnia is a poet of the night,
a poet of raging oceans,
confused emotions,
melancholy intestines,
hormone-imbalances,
& gross impurities of body & mind.

bestiary of thought
filled with the gods i must have forgotten
becoming
monsters in the closet
(gay monsters)
egrets, emus,
lions, whales,
cross-porpoises,
angry elephants
and one horny rhinoceros.

a zoo of the living
forgotten, but still not forgiving
today's unlucky breaks,
mistakes,
my debts,
regrets,
pseudo-sexual bets,
made once upon forgotten time
by the foes or friends of my subconscious mind
that i'm still trying to win.

vagaries of desire
vaginas & breasts & a penis

conspire
afraid of getting wet
or hard
except in dreams.

lies & simulations,
imagined situations,
catharsis
like transcontinental current-seas
libidinal economies,
blood-let,
bed-wet
dream-sweat,
can't get
dry in these pools of thought

the dream looms
but never visits
my sedentary soul
to unearth my unfathomable.

the somewhere soils
that can predict
when my over-processed memories
will stop their photosynthesis,
unearth, rewind
& reverse my daytime-lusts
and just respire.

to breathe or not to breathe--
is that the question?

relax the body's muscles
& the tension in the jaw & forehead.
focus on the inner-eye?

but no technique,
technology,
sleep therapy or pill
will ever be
the whole solution.

because the solution is
balance,
order &
harmony.

throughout
my will & lusts,
my social consciousness,
intestines, lymph-nodes,
conscience, & my soul--

in short,
for my whole life world
the life-achievement of
world-peace.

my world laid to rest
having paid the price of sleep.

world-order.

until then,
sleep disorder.

XMEN

we mutants walk among you,
freakazoids,
whose DNA is different

NOW,

whose powers are unlike any
humankind has ever seen.

yeah, we're the freaks
who generated the mystique of MTV,
& sucked at teats
whose milk was laced
with scooby-doo
& the brady bunch.

& of course, we went to church
because our folks were raised in the 1950's,
before hugh hefner & madonna.

& our grade-school marms were flower kids
who read foucault in grad-school.
& we lived
through star wars,
& the end of cold wars
& cabinets full of x-files
that gathered dust
while we were out
jumping our BMXs
& playing our x-games
& our ATARIs
& other proto-x-boxes.

& our unique
cerebro-cortical disorders
can be explained by the fact
that the cable guy forgot,
& hard-wired the gateway
straight to our brains,
direct-connecting the pipeline of
our 3rd-generation TVs
into our heads,

transforming us

into the psycho-cyclopses we've become,
whose single mental eye
can never sleep, but, ever-hungry, seeks
new blue-screen chimeras
of michael-jackson-"thriller"-status
& visions of new superstars
to disco-dance
in our groovy-to-the-max head-rooms...
with their marlboros, & brat packs,
& big screens, & smoke-machines
blowing a mental fog
that blinds us to the sinister fact that
we live a rogue existence,
no more than a fool's gambit,
while some rough beast
asleep in our subconscious
slouches toward hollywood to be born.

but we don't care.
we live in our minds.
& our very best friends are the images we find there
of ralph maccio & jon bon jovi,
& the new swatch watch we've got to have,
& the power of greyskull.

& the red ropes of
this red carpet,
über-posh party
of pop icons
& pop-up ads
& soda pop
& popcorn consumerism,
are already too overpopulated
with the demons of
our dreams & discontents
to admit the memory
that it was *our* grandparents who saw
the nightmare of the holocaust,
& the storm of normandy,
& a whole apocalypse of shattered lives...

& it was *our* grandfathers who walked,
dream-like, like broken men,
naked & with barefoot souls
through the ashes & coals of auschwitz
& the 6 million jews who would have no jubilee...

...as the final bastion of hope
for what could have been humanity
lay razed & smoldering there.

but what is that to us?
we, like a phoenix, rise up
from our primal stardust, because

    our generation is

FOREVER.

    that's right.
    we've changed with the times.
    & we were there for the epiphany, just
    like you,
    when trinity & neo kissed—
    we worshipped too,
    at the theater.

    & we may not be as "rad" as all that,
    but we're still "cool."

    so what does it matter,
    then, about our up-bringing,
    & all the concrete symbols we imbibed—
    the strange, intoxicating brew
    uniquely mixed & blended to our cultural
    unconscious?

    do all these fleeting symbols
    with which we feel affinity
    embody our identity?

    we might as well have worshipped
    zeus or marduk or osiris!
    the symbols change,
    but every age
    conceals the same vitality.

    doesn't it?

& what does it mean that
our gene-ration,
our generation is "x" or "y" or "z"?
of course our chromosomes are fated,

but in our minds we're free! ...right?

...well, even if our minds are free,
we can't escape our bodies....
    maybe we'll live to be 80. maybe
    we'll be forgotten. maybe

        our generation is

FOR-NEVER.

& all our mid-life crises,
medicaids & mausoleums
are just tiny specks
on the timeline of world events,
insignificant as dead skin-paste
on a '68 nickel.

   & we thrive... & we strive...
      till history puts its hex,
      its dark & final X,
      upon our names & generation.

   to strive, exist,
   to be or not to be
smothered by the cold, uncaring hands
of a history that doesn't give a fuck.

      to it, we're just the next
      sad little bit of code
      in the program of man's de-volution;

      or the next fresh load
      of bio-hazardous human waste
      placed on the trash-heaps of time;

      the newest food for future anthropologists,
      & the maggots,
      & historians,
      & nightcrawlers,
      & leeches
      of the academies to come,

asking themselves what powers we had,
& telling their myths about stuff that we did,
but wondering still in the back of their heads:

"who was the author?"
was it we? or 1990? or all of human history?
we are the XMEN.

christmas spirit

the time of year
for christmas cheer
& christmas spirit
comes.

what is the "christmas spirit"?
maybe it's baby jesus in a bed.

or maybe maxing credit cards
until the corporate monster's fed.

or maybe reminiscing with "the fam"
with eggnog generously spiked
so nobody remembers what is said.

god, pleasure, wealth, & love.

(never alone, but always
some combination thereof)—
these are the only motives that our
childish, lovestruck, undersexed, & money-grubbing culture
knows.

these motives are façades
for the endangered species: LIFE.

although they masquerade as truth,
they are vizards our organisms wear;
the games we play in leisuretime,
ideologies, idolatries,
usurping a humanity
so nearly extinct
that it can barely whisper
from its deathbed.

& all our objects,
grand designs,
our institutions, alcazars, & goods—

these are but indices of
our facile values & existence,
our infantile *raison d'être*.

florist & retail store,

bookshop & bakery,
skyscraper, university,
cathedral, synagogue, & mosque—

these are but signs & symptoms
for some amalgam of impeti—
built, produced, & circulating wares;
false factories that iterate

god, pleasure, wealth, & love.

what is the "christmas spirit"?

if "christmas" is a name
whose meaning changes with the years,
the question must be put historically.

& for our puerile place in time,
the question is the same:

what is the "human spirit"?

donkey

the circle of eager humans
clubs in hand
surround
the lifeless body of
the beast of burden,
its insides spilled out
onto the cold, hard earth:

man's mastery
over the brutes
symbolized here
by children
laughing, gazing on
the broken body
of the donkey
of paper-maché.

army

in this war
we're the spies
we private eyes
trade
excuses for our greed.
& lust is the need
of the hour
where power's
the game that is played
& the prayer that is prayed
in the name of love.

& nobody wins
until everyone's fought
until everyone's bought
until everyone's "ought"
becomes the "is"
of
the public opinion poll.

polls
polarize
& mobilize
& enlist our existence
& our thoughts
& our legs
into the armed forces
of the fascist regime
of today's
to-do list.

ants
bumping into each other
in the night
rubbing our bodies
against each other
in seedy beds
of earth

forgetting that
we all come
into the same hole.

out of the same hole.

rubbing antennae
bumping into each other
in the daylight
on a crowded street
carrying burdens
for the same queen
the same regime

rubbing shoulders
trading pheromones
trading identities

rubbing off
on one another until
we become
a world of
carbon copies,
all of us
bottom copies
on the back
of bank deposit slips.

in a world
that can only be
described as
mutual masturbation
we all come at once
to the same
conclusions.

narcissus

open your eyes.
what do you see?

cars, coffee-shops, pages & people.
fast food, fashion, cash, & tv screens.

because the eye sees what the hands make.
& the eyes become what they see.

so our eyes become technologies,
projects, manipulations, simulations, hallucinations,
reflections… where
eye mirrors eye.
i mirrors i.
eye for eye.
i for i.

trading,
becoming (art),
traded (art).
art officials,
artifice aficionados,
reproducing ourselves,
& becoming imitations & replications
of each other

in which
i mimic you & you mimic me
until we become each other's apes, and
copies of copies of copies of copies…

indefinitely.
& the eyes do not see
the seeds become trees
& the stars & the seas
& the magma hardening into mountains,
& the lioness covering her kill with debris.

& the eyes do not view
the cacophonous zoo,
or the square root of two,
or the essence of you,

since they're fixed

on their own reflection
in the alternate eyes of their secret ad-mirrors,
in the infinite hallway of self-images,
in the self-outside-of-self
that is both master and slave,
the labyrinth
whose bait is
        the truth & the beauty,
        the love & the good
        of its own
                image
                      that keeps on repeating itself
                      in an infinite line...
                      till it seems like
        the image of god
        to the eyes
of the mind.

what do i mean?

this is my truth in action:

i have sexual thoughts about almost everyone
i meet.
it's part of how i size them up.
& my irony
is that pain begets pain
and power, power.
and i cope with my past
through desire.

& the walls are thick
that hold me inside,
& i might take a risk
& i might be denied,
but i try.

i try to find fellow creators.
& if my existence creates devotees
i grow sad,
like god's disappointment
when he couldn't fuck what he made
because he created inferiors
& zombies
& mindless admirers,
sending him mind-numbing
submissions
whose subtext reads:
YOU CANNOT BE LOVED.

it's not you, it's me.

& sometimes
i'm tired and dusty
like an old pair of feet
that dance to your rhythm
like the infinite beat
of my pain.

& my pleasure's there too
loving
& enchanted
& insecure
like any soul-nudist

at war
with obsessive thoughts
& needs
& overflowing love
outpoured.
& true is how i treat you.

>   the lion roars
>   the child sings
>   the camel weeps
>   tomorrow brings
>   a change.

it's all about rhythm.
hit me at the right time
& i'll re-evaluate your values.
i'll rock your world.
i'm not a neophyte.
i'm a connoisseur of existence.

& i always change
inside
& out
& even my anxieties
& doubts
make the world a better place.

because

i say what i think.
& honesty's my policy
worldwide
& inside my intricate web
of feelings
& thoughts
& detachments
& engagements.

& you say
that to bring what's inside to symbols
is absurd
when all of my senses are
flirting with yours
and the mystery is there
but to bring it to words
seems insane.

& maybe it's true.
maybe
i surf my id
like the internet,
google
a million ways to say what i feel,
& i click the first one
i think links
to my goals.

is that honesty's game?

deploying
honest metaphors,
mercenaries of pragmatism,
getting me what i want?

i will tell you what I want.

i want something beautiful.

so i will make my words and actions beautiful and good.
and i will give them to you as a gift.
and if you resonate,
you will call them true.

being, barred

the silence deafens
where inaudible screams translate to
voice-boxes muted.
some things cannot be said.

the air is still
with invisible restraints of soul.
life itself is for living.

of course, there are the customary unseen
guardrails, handrails, & turnstiles of being--
smiles and handshakes,
transactions--

pay the starbucks barista your cash,
smile,
politely take your change,
and wait for your coffee.

get a career,
get an apartment,
have acquaintances,
have hobbies,
have opinions.

of course.

like the deer's paths in the forest
or the dolphin's migration routes
through the sea,
such bio-ruts are to be expected.

but there is something else.

in the silence.
in the stillness.

being. barred.

a prison
known only by yearning.

desire's hands, privation's cuffs.

your only idea
and
your only pen, out of ink.

definition

how do definitions
finitize
differently
in dictionaries
&
in my life?

...a question of environment.

milieus fertilize
far more than
concept-gardens
or leaves of idio-lexicons.

finite functions
float among
dendrites,
valences,
ferris-wheel spokes,
dark chocolate aromas,
hugs,
kisses,
favorite songs,
familiar bonds,
soothing blues & therapeutic suns--
whatever entries make me definite.

i make sense.

i am a definition.
the ever-changing world, my
dictionary.

rotflmao mentalese

somniloquent visions of
hip-hop blogospheres
trip out doggs with weird mirror-neurons:
sword-plowshares circulate,
electric ligersporks,
misplaced madre-fires,
piss-faced padre-mires,
cadre-desires,
godplay-rewires,
dad-mods
& mom-morphs
pre-figure
friend requests,
hero lists,
faith, hope, & transcription errors
for futures whose
open windows
add to favorites
(point-click & cut & paste)--
it's all about possession
& saving face.

where dasein-icons *represent*,
ontology asks only:
whose?
&
how used?
spilled out by succulent virtual lips
in pay-per-click-acceptance-ese,
& copyleft identities
for now called
'mine,'
& 'hers,'
& 'his.'

locusts chew stems
on cannabis weeds
past markets,
report cards,
& titles & deeds,
leading lives
of use-value,
as easy as
enumerating sheep.

the greener grass
has grown
under the fence.

hey look!
i photoshopped my id
onto your ego.

TTYL.

starstruck

medusa's in the mirror
starstruck
where everyone thinks it's
about themselves.

self-loving
self-hating celebrities
of self-consciousness
in long-term
love-hate
self-relationships
are first to
get the question
mirrors ask:

"aren't you somebody?"

goddesses long to be whores
whose doors open only to fools
who refuse to worship,
iconoclasts who smash the
mirrors & clichés of the subconscious,
fearless of the fabled
7 years bad luck.

gods reward tenacity, not piety.

submission is its own reward…

…where conformity is self-absorption
& self-deprecation is a synonym for
ordinary values,

the order of things
is kept intact
by the prostrate paralytics
of the zodiac.

ode to truth

in all of your beauty,
your approach is like lightning.
& you are not mad,
but are coherent & sticky,
like lava & oatmeal—
    in all of your wholeness,
        your wonders are woven together.
& in you are born all the tongues of the earth.
with your keen correspondence,
you speak with the world as its intimate friend.

when i see you commune with the cliffs & the ocean
& man's relics
& all manner of natural objects,
i am tempted to call you "objective."
but you object,
because i, too, am your subject,
when you steal in by night
as a fire & a riddling dancer
& leave me with questions,
but never with answers.

or by day,
when your waters
diffuse all my projects & feelings,
& i am tempted to call you "subjective,"
you remind me with stones
& with stars & with libraries
that my mind
& men's words
are but two of your infinite quarters.

then you beam over me,
with the smile of a muse and a mentor,
when you see me converse with my friends,
or go out to work or to play,
since all of my actions & dealings & deepest desires
        betray the fond stroke of your tutelage.

at rest, in the stillness,
in the shadows of evening,
you uncover my uttermost meaning.

and so, my beloved,

i give myself to your study.
but not like the scholarly, sterile & proud archaeologists,
whose insecure fingers probe into your surface,
as into the closed account of the past,
with precision & accuracy & correctness,
debating your forms & formations.
        in your fullness, you let them devour your crumbs & dry crusts.
you laugh in your magma
as they measure the height of your mountains,
because, as a joke, you deliberately left them
these strange lithographs of your lava's late presence.

so i will not seek you
alone
in stone tablets,
in the quarrelsome fixing of "right" & "wrong" values,
in the saying of "yes" and of "no"—

because by your wind & your water & fire,
you prove that you also require
the love of a meteorologist.

& so, like a lover, i study your forces,
your great mighty acts
& dread deeds.

and my rigor will be
to determine your ways in the depths of the water,
& the movement of stars & your eyes,
& which way the winds of your heart may be blowing...

...& whether the brink
of the day that is dawning
brings anew your cold snows,
or dark storms,
or warm sunshine—
once again to the world
and my life.

libidinal labels

libidinal labels
are libel, are liable
to come from the bible
or some psycho-babel...
but somehow they're able
(like cain) to turn tables
of cravings & gavels,
behaviors we dabble in,
ravings unraveled,
& reveries traveled,
    because we would *rather*
    be bound to the blathering
    id of our fathers
    & sisters & brothers,
    whose mind-numbing chatter
    on lecherous matters
    continues to rattle
    around in the battle
    of sexes, where cattle,
    in herds, chase their habits;
    conceiving like rabbits,
    to churn out their babies...
...*than* realize that maybe
we're just stored-up labor
that burdens our neighbors
who just want to savor
the hot lustful flavor
of life without fables
of saviors in stables
or other such libel
that comes from the bible
or some psycho-babel,
that darkly we're able
to trace on time's table
to piles of unstable
libidinal labels.

punctuality for naked souls

even though
no one told you where to
close the
parentheses
on

"present company excluded,"

the scientists of your paranoia
hung up their labcoats,
too tired to
analyze subtexts for implicatures,
leaving
your wounded wit-machines to wonder:

"why would he choose to score THAT way?"

leaving
you
side-split
fireside
drunk-laughing
bottle-passing
with the security-guards of my being
until you said,

"let's get our souls naked and see what happens."

no one says "no"
after a soul-baring session.

but apple-fish cosmotini intestines
reserve the right to say

"i don't care"

or

"always"

afterwards
because
after words,
as spirits wane

to the smoke of informal
inflections,

the sea turns over in its
bed
to dream again
the oneness
of our
one.

pay attention

whatever people see & hear,
focus & fixate on,
& spend their time thinking about...
...becomes the world.

publics form opinions.

& propagandas
(cinema & media agendas)
bark orders
to direct
our inward eyes.

but we are not their victims.

what we notice
is *our* responsibility.

what we think about
is *our* responsibility.

we form thought-habits,
familiar *loci* in our mindscape—
synapse-superhighways,
loops in our circuitry,
watering holes,
pissed-on trees &
vomit
to which our hounds of thought return.

these common places,
psycho-stomping-grounds,
& visibilities
dictate
legislation,
salaries of sex symbols,
fetishes & fashion trends,
theologies,
neologies,
& pseudo-academic disciplines.

norms & institutions outside,
mental haunts inside.

climates of opinion
generating culture-storms.

civilization
(our form of life)
a map to the
topography of our attention.

mood music

not a day goes by
that i don't make
a million little choices
that alter the course of my life.

      & sometimes i make big choices.

& everything
i say & do,
i do
amid a slew
of shifting moods & mental states...

...what was it
that i *said* when i was tipsy?
or *did* when i was horny?
or *planned* when i was happy?
what was it i *decided* when i was hyper?
or *chose* when i was overwhelmed?

& was it the same "i" who did these things?
...or is there a different "i"
for each mood & attitude?

...then i could say,
"*happy-i* ate the broccoli,
while *worried-i* paid the bills...
then *cranky-i* talked on the phone
until *tired-i* drifted to sleep."

then i would be a schizophrenic,
and a magical river
that cannot be stepped in twice.

      then i would be
      a great-swirling tide & desultory breeze;
      a mad, morphing landscape & volatile fire;

      & i could be solid, or liquid, or air.
      & as the air, gale-force or gust.

      & though yesterday-i may have been your best friend,
      still, today-i may be your worst enemy.
      & i'd warn you

        that sometimes your sails should beware of my waters.

as the earth, i would find
the lost art of existence,
& the hidden attunement by which
i become what i eat—
by which my moods & mental states
succumb to the fate of my diet & exercise,
my regimens & rituals—
physical, mental & social.

& in this light, i would see
that my everyday moods
are part of the
fiery wisdom & word
that steers all-things
through all-things
in the great-swirling world of my life.

on wave, wormhole, & wind

wormholes & blackholes congregate.
spacetime wants to be travelled
like wind wants to be sailed.

time's molecules are sticky & cohere
like air-masses that rush
& rarify to fill a void;
or crush, condense,
& join high-pressure fronts.

galactic winds of spacetime blow
when, low to high or high to low,
its matter, energy & light
condense & rarify.

the universe is breathing.

we would not want to meet
a wormhole
    any more than
           a tornado;
a blackhole
    any more than
           a hurricane.

but not all weather is severe.

we live a placid spacetime
that moves about as much
as air displaced
by candleflames.

still,
such micro-flows
encode
astral apparition &
information from afar.

our ghosts & muses ride these tiny gusts.

      they say
      butterfly wings in mexico
      make monsoons in malaysia.

& even ocean currents & jetstreams
derive their cumulative force
from
the whirling whims
& eddy-dances
of their micro-vectors.

    just so, the chaos of these three is one:
    spacetime & air & particle.

    one becoming swirls
    through the strong & weak symphonies of superstrings,
    through sticky magnetisms of spacetime,
    & the gravities that give us wind & wave.

i said everything

i said everything that i wanted to say
since i went down that way
anymore i don't pay
attention to the words
it's absurd
like a bird
that flies into a window
the pain
is intense
and the reign
in the brain
of a madness
that laughs
in the mouths of the dying
at the joke
that they're already dead

amid the chaos of routinely

        amid the chaos of routinely
                tilts the green
            on the screen
        in the dream
          of an everyday conversation
    somewhat dark in its wise
                to the creamy-white eyes
of the seemingly poet careening

    i slip in for the salt of a visit

                what i bring
                    to the drowsy
                pool-party
       are the weapons of silence
                  for the scream,
"he's got guns that nobody else is deploying!"

as the wind on the overcast carnivalesque
                  wins the need
              for a smoke
          ...swimmingly...
        ...a remember...

& who does it take for the strange of the mirror of went?

                      with a
                  sad final glass
    the reflect on a crown on a clown

              with meticulous rules for
                forgetting
          for the you
            of identification cards
                      in
                  which
          the seed of the soul
                is implanted
    as if into the world of a question
        of i.

the cat

i have almost made a companion
of the feral cat

that lives in my basement.

we respect each other's
lives at a distance.

today my feline friend is watching
the smoke pour off my cigarette
with her intelligent eyes.

she may one day die of curiosity
or i of cancer,

but in this moment,
we both learn
the essence of conscience:
the feeling
that we are being watched
by the eyes of another
who is
both pure and wise.

so dies eidos

in a graveyard
that defies gravity,
corpses in the sky
like dead ideas
stick to my bathroom ceiling--
fruit flies.

The Node Not Taken

Two nodes diverged in a neural knot,
And sorry I could not charge them both
And be one Impulse, I forgot
The left, turned right, and made a Thought,
A Choice that led to Memory growth.

But part of my impeded flow
Went traveling down the other spur.
Its ohm-like after-feelings whirred,
For where no Thought would ever go,
Somehow a trace was registered.

The trail I blazed is fortified,
The synapse superhighway paved.
The other trail has long since died,
But in the shady trees roadside,
Faint phantom-feelings haunt its grave.

New currents will program my lungs to sigh
Somewhere ages and ages hence:
Two nodes diverged in a brain, and I,
Took one of them, not asking why—
And that has made all the difference.

bellagio
(beautiful ease)

the velvet distance
of spectacular vaginas
& pious speed-boats
crumbles as it creates
a galaxy of asterisks,
a gamble,
astonishingly simple,
the gleam of neon
in the eye of the coyote.

even though

in the moonlight,
the cardboard cylinder
with shreds of toilet paper
from the old roll
is still hanging there
by the spring-loaded centerpiece,
sitting there
between the two plastic arms
that are screwed into the wall...
even though
the new roll is on top of it,
almost halfway finished;

even though
it's 4am
and i'm drunk off my ass,
i undo the spring-loaded centerpiece
and take off the old cylinder
and put the new roll
back onto the wall--

even though
she was the one
who finished the old roll
and it should have been her job,
and
even though
it wouldn't have taken that much effort;
even though
i can't figure out
why she can never remember
or why she is so lazy;

even though
i'll probably never tell her
about what happened tonight
at 4am,
when i was drunk
and changed the roll for her,
because i love her
and really,
it's not that big a deal.

friend

what not to ask
is not a kitten
inside an apartment
it is a crosswalk
with women standing by
waiting
not a movie theater
but perhaps
a metropolis
or a desert
if only i could see the clock
ticking
i could explain to you
what imagination
is for

imaginary action figures

i sat by Rosa Parks in economy class,
too tired to network with Axel Rose.
my natural self committed suicide
in the airport bathroom
with some hairgel & accessories
& i emerged resurrected as Brad Pitt.
Socrates called the cell,
& i had to put Gandhi on hold.
CNN reported that
Howard Hughes had Karl Marx committed.
Jesus wept.
T.S. Eliot was in a talkative mood.
Hugh Hefner just sat there smoking.

impromptu

summon your sorrows,
dressed in pajamas,
laugh
as they drop through
solitary skies,
the modest jungles of the stomach,
eyelid movie-screens,
& untainted alarm-clocks
with hands of greek goddesses,
droning
intricate & tuneless.

it's all about you babe

it's all about you, babe.
keep talkin'.
i'll just listen
to the words,
& to the light in your eyes,
& how you are coping with the pain.
& maybe i'll penetrate
the conversation later
with banalities about myself
to dominate you
with the empty intrusion
of my imperial weather updates
& maybe i will share with you
how i feel more like a man now
after a few moments of enlightenment,
how i am learning to externalize my insecurities
& my feelings of inadequacy
instead of hiding behind them
and how i even desire different things now...
...or maybe i'll just listen.
after all,
it's all about you, babe.

name-brand candy

for us
life is like
name-brand candy.

we buy it,
stick it in our mouth,
and suck on it.

and it's sweet.
and then,
it's gone.

and no one
is
the wiser.

and someone
is
a little
richer.

ode to my parents

one can never BE enough for one's parents.
mom,
dad--
i can never be enough for you.

but
i will always be FOR you,
and just enough for you,
and just right,
in the paradox
of being
you and not-you,

of being
an incarnation of your genes,
your values,
your way of thinking,
your hopes,
your dreams --
a combination --
a waking, breathing possibility -
YOUR possibility (one of many),
your miracle,
your ACTUALITY,
actualized into a new generation -
into a LIFE -
(my life?
your life?)
your life in me.

and
in my veins,
your blood.

and
in my face,
your reflection,
your mirror.

it's not just
that WORDS cannot express
my feeling
or my gratitude,
or my desire to please you

or my urge to help you...

my LIFE cannot express it.

but,
to you,
i will always express it,
perfectly,
with eyebrows and intonations.

and
while my existence
may be

an infinite debt

that i owe you,
you do not think of repayment.
you do not ask for installments.

(after all,
what sum could say,
"thanks, mom and dad.
thanks for having me"?)

your love is
beyond
having or
owing or
owning or
praise.

you gave.

and for that,
i love you.

omen

rest sleepers
for these are not my primary buttocks
extract!
extract!
extraction is for those who have no interest in sanity
every tooth extracted
every hand severed
the primal fear of failing
falling
fathers

perfection

i bring perfection to the grid
the power of suggestion
the power of love
an entrance entertained
in the abyss
of the moment
that is everything
thinking reality
breathing the feeling
traversing distinctions
like rows of cotton
it is a style of living
tensed and wandering
through the tongues of many peoples
a loss of personal history
of world history
insofar as it is mine
the night
whose light is nature
behind the artificial party
behind the games
and the rules
a connection
intense & unsevered
answering my
unasked question.

persuasion

persuasion is vibration
& rhythm is decision
blindness an intricacy of perception
an exquisite temptation
a primal dishonesty
the original sin of the body.
i am a serpent
even now
tempting you with finitudes
deluding your will
undermining your innocence
with the succulence of my vowels.
shoot me in the face!
shoot me now!
and slay the oldest dragon.

politics of friendship

i'm not expecting profound revelations
bring me your unbridled unhesitations

don't bring me your poor & unkempt huddled masses
unwashed beggars & down-trodden derelicts

i don't have wine
and i'm all out of chronic

i am not your statue of liberty
and you are not mine

be your own free country
and in your own time

be yourself

my congress is in session
i've gotta go

you have some good policies

see you next spring
in geneva

possession

the death of possessions
when credit malfunctions
and the medical malpractice suit
yield to
the market growth
and fluctuation
of achievement
bought and sold
in the world of ego and academia
the right to dictate our whims
to the deferential bowing of peers
naked sand and silk
flowing in the breeze
like a fleeting glimpse
of temporary pleasure
the soft temptation of whores
and merlot
that bites us
like the gristle
between the teeth
of our grinding expectations
a steak of disappointment
all too satisfying
for a few moments
of beautiful indulgence

presence

i write in your presence
& a flock of insecurities
take flight
at the sound of the fox's paw
blood and water
the depth of dna as cliche
ours
the tempestuous relation
of love deconstructed
in the silver overcoming
this is the kingdom
and you are
my fathers
my sisters
my brothers
my mothers
fuck derrida!
we spirit dionysus
just for presence
three pale antichrists
uncut by aspirations
clouds
not
pyramids
a pair of meaningless panties on the bedpost.

re: hi!

i sent a mentality
in your direction
a bona fide erection
vocal inflection
dissection
of my soul
into words
into ones
and zeros
and infinities
and

into cyberspace
to flamenco
through the vast
and the flames
in the skirt
of an orbital game
where
what hides
is
as hot
as what's hidden

forbidden fruit

flirting with codes
email a la mode

of communication
to clothe
my bare

body of meaning

roxanne & mephistopheles

your pimp
is a pimple,
tootsie:
POP!
lollygagging
on cradle pillows,
dreamy
electric seawaters:

you have swallowed
too much forgiveness.

selling your see-shell,
saving--
"bon voyage!"--
to sail from soul.
the shores have too much sunlight.
the shells bake there.

but you were born amid sumptuous waves.

on moonlit nights,
the abyss still seems like a purple noun,
a dark father,
the subject of your economic sentence.

there is much water in you.

your devil's detail
conjugates the tidal question:
do breakers have sad histories?
or is the crush
just now:
a free-fall
for
your mollusk-heart?

sex party

...or maybe it was something
about the newness of the situation
everyone was fucking
and i couldn't get it up
usually i like porn
i like to watch
usually
but it just felt like
watching
the discovery channel
or the history channel
do they even have a channel
for people fucking?
like brute facts
introducing themselves
as the way things are
unencumbered by amorous afterglows
thrusting through all of my senses
like humanesque blobs
like a gun without a trigger
the naked humanity
was as exciting as seeing
myself
naked in the mirror
i didn't feel conflicted
or inhibited or repressed
i didn't feel anything
at times
i felt something
when will got the best of want
it was a beautiful experiment
just before i had fought with words
with my lover
we made up
and she became everything again
she became everything
and my cock got big
and that was fun
fun
fun
more fun than ever
i came
and then it was over
and the world didn't change

i didn't set sail
my lover remained my lover
my partners
objects
you
the most beautiful thing of all
was making love
next to you both
when our bodies would touch
seeing you
seeing us
where our bodies made their debuts
as such.

sunshine

truth is like weather.
it's always there,
but it's not the same everywhere.

the devil's warrior

dare to think
in the absence of interpretation
unhindered by deliberation
moving between
the arbitrary transferences
that motivate self-doubt
be the devil's warrior
against the status quo
the deaf ears
that only hear the audible
erase the dictionaries
the sterile phalluses of semblance
erase them with death.

the force

your soul walks naked
in your eyes,
aphrodite--
unashamed,
dangerous,
dancing through the world,
glancing about,
slicing through the souls
of the men
that your eyes fall on,
like a jedi sword
through grapefruit.

fearless,
full of passion
and love for humankind,
overflowing,
giving--

without pretense,
without defense,
your pupils penetrate
aggressively,
cutting through
any soul that is not
strong and pure and true.

inadvertently your gaze
kills them--
the ones who, like icarus,
come too close.

but when your eyes met mine,
our souls met

resistance,

a low electric hum,

that neither of us expected.
it had been so long.

the only poetry

the most important thing in poetry is honesty:
honesty with the world and with ourselves.
and we can be
honest or dishonest
without ever knowing it,
but never against our will.

the expression is everything.

and this is the most important thing:
honesty is thorough.
do not think that you can be
honest in content
without being honest
in rhythm and rhyme.

honesty is the only poetry.

it is an art form.

if this is true of poetry
it is because
it is true
of life.

this is a poem

this is a poem.
this is ink on a page.

i am an artist.
i am a poet.

this proves it.
this embodies my creativity.

this is the problem of reference.
this is the problem of transference.
this is the problem of demonstrative pronouns.

this is the feeling of becoming an object.
this is the feeling of dying.
this is frustration.

this is a soulflashing moment of transcendence.
this is bliss.

i am art.
i am this poem.

touch

i want you to take something
beautiful from me
take something from out of the ugliness
out of the thingliness
from the slavery to conceit
and circumstance
a feather
or an anthem
the utter sanity
of the experience of chocolate
and if i am embarrassed later
to have been eaten
remind me
that it was meant to be
and i will nevermore feel ridiculous
when you touch my skin

ii.

in & out

a hidden word

a hidden word inside my heart and head,
the answer to my life, my guiding thread.
whisper it:
and i know my way through the maze.

this word is not like other words
i speak when with acquaintances,
it's never
wrong, nor imprecise, nor a facade.

this word cannot be uttered,
it's much more like a smile.
smile at me:
and it sings across my face.

a single word, a thought, a sign,
my feelings and my hopes align.
find it:
and i will find myself in you.

abecedarius of compliments

alluring & adept
bold & bestial
cuddly & clever
daring & demure

erotic & elegant
fleshy & forlorn
grunting & glam
hot & headstrong

intriguing & informed
judicious & jazzy
kinesthetic & keen
lascivious & lean

magnanimous & mindful
nomadic & nonpareil
observant & original
passionate & pure

quixotic & quiescent
refined & reticent
savory & sweet
thrilling & tame

unusual & unscripted
virtuous & veiled
wily & wild
xenophilic & xoanonic

youthful & yearning
zealous & zen

dream
(a.k.a. life is a journey)

it's espionage
& under the sheets
is just a hiding place.
fucking just passes the time.

it's all about pleasure
till i can't find your g...
that,
that sends us running
naked
from construction workers
& people in hummers
& boats.

where are our friends?
we might miss the journey.
they see us. we are out of reach.

we caused the accident.
i will remember your red hair.
will you remember me?
SLEEP.
we can no longer sing to our rings
to empower them.

five red apples

the rarified air of theory
investigates these five red apples
as though they were mathematical objects,
colorless, odorless,
ready to take their invisible place
in the architecture of some crystalline heaven,

far from the marketplace hullabaloo,

the jolly old woman
who steps on your shoe accidentally;
soft wind,
bright sunshine,
rustling leaves;
subtle twitches at mouth-corners,
the quick eyes,
& quicker rhetoric
of the street-hustler hocking his wares...

and above all,
the sensuous curve of each orb,

ripe reds,
& the weight of their water:
the saliva
that squirts
on its own
at their succulent fragrance.

heartbeats

love is a one-hour trip to the louvre
in which you are expected
to compare yourself
with all its artifacts and relics,
and emerge with a singular comprehension
of who you are.

love is a book of poems
you wrote years ago
which, when you look back over them,
seem foreign.

love is a knock on your door,
an invitation
to the most improbable cup of coffee.

if only there were words for such honesty,
if only such honesty for words,
love would lie down next to you
and never leave.

ode to an oyster

dream, oyster,
rocked by your cradle, the sea...

until the aliens come,
organisms from the air universe
with false ocean-bodies.
land-animals. predators.

this is worse than a nightmare:
they are here for you.

your shell was not built for this.

your love, your care,
your projects & your pride,
your salty powers & sandy responsibility--
none of these can save you now.

the iron implements are set.

you will crack.

the chef is already slicing lemons.

ode to bikinis and insecurities

under the weather
is an understatement

who wants to be
misunderstood
especially
undressed?

once there was sunshine

i forget if it was the amalfi coast
or santa monica

your mind is a relic
feelings don't leave skeletons

generation
has always been a problem

as a woman
of course you pluck your eyebrows

first it was thongs

waistlines dropped
with barometric peer pressure

now fewer and fewer
even wear
underwear

Sein zum Tode

DEATH is not a razor
slashing soles
on moonlit beaches,
bled,
brain bramble-bushed,
sung by
achromatic-open-vowel-boy-choir
modulations.

if this were death,
no one would embrace it.

because its scissor-tricks are
breast-strokes winging over waters,
DEATH glides
and surveys,
with the strength of a predator,
full-bellied.

DEATH is the impotence
of omnipotence —
a universe of possibility
contracted to a single point.

in a word,
(but only here & now),
it's you.

in this,
                (attention:oversight)
death is de-cision
and
de-cision is death.

passionfruit

is it too much to ask
for your facts
not your politics
as my fingertips caress
the base of your skull
through your hair
not to hear
some distinction
between *de facto*
and *de jure*

play the game
with everyone else

win

but sing to me
a lullaby

so that when we sleep
our bodies
will inherit
the blue sky

anthem

curious upright beast
waddling along on two legs
soft flesh
straddling genitals
no longer mysterious
still covered by cloth
having
sprung from embryo
learned language
worn by work
by dreams
classed by money
by style
by pride
still crying out inside
"i am vulnerable!"
"i am mortal!"

do

roll out the red carpet
for your nightmares
as the flower opens petals
toward the dawn,
turn yourself in
to the world.

touch the stovetops of your being
make love,
one by one,
to your demons,
your greatest sages.

there is no magic here,
no logic you can learn in school.
here you will die
and be born
in the same act
to the music of your choosing.

when you're out of painkillers,
make the world your soundtrack.
soundtrack the world
& stumble on unsturdy legs
into the great dance to

DO!

or just sit there
till the grave
finds your flesh
unsavory.

strum

strum through the manual
life has to offer
the merry-go-round
of life-o-rama
petals & snocones
for puppycat
nostalgia
or xylophones
rusting
undersea
whisper
"change!"
"change!"
break eggs over teflon
unless your heart hurts
devour yolks
by bookcases
& bigscreens
for desire's holiday between
the space between
alarm clocks swimming
yelling
"change!"
"change!"

liquid courage

oatmeal stout slides down the gullet
as the mood of the space
slowly but surely
metamorphosizes.

the light becomes more possible.
each distance ripens.
the air grows dense with happiness.

what left is tangible too,
what is leaving:
the demon of the ordinary.

& as the fog of inhibition flees,
conversations with strangers commence.

words slip through lips,
smiles.

history has finally grown
honest.

on dice & victory

especially at times like these,
i think you will agree,
there will be a difference
between strong & sad--
if strong is mistaken often enough for essential
where screaming or a sword or teeth or repetition
is the soundest syllogism
& everyone says: GO, GO, GO!
as if traveling were primary or Being proper.

trade names with something common or inanimate
inadequate or cavalier--
weapons or weapons or
tools or tools
to connect with subtexts,
penises, puzzles,
& the size of hat brims
as an index of history
of a dimensionality
waiting to possess
your soul forever,
to forestall some chemical reaction,
for life at absolute zero
or consciousness at lightspeed
since

confusion is the absence of the usual irony.

heartcry

give me something
before you go
some piece of you

> a token
> a sacrament
> a ruby

make me a star
in your night sky

> a photograph
> a lock of hair
> a ring

some delusional object
that says i am not forsaken

as it goes

the earth shits diamonds
we shit fertilizer
aphids, sugar.

this is the cosmos,
the flow
of the great river:

each time it takes,
it transforms
and leaves a gift
behind it

as it goes.

roses

death is passive
life is active
grammar is god
& we are but pawns in a game
that we don't understand.

hearts weep in barcelona
for towels that hang
on clotheslines
outside the poorman's window
amid rolling hills,
spanish solely
by virtue of the fact
that they hang over spain.

these are the true flags
that give even tigers pause.

& for all the poet cafés
& cantinas
for all the smiling young virgins named maria
who danced beneath flamenco dresses,
there is always
a man & a woman.

there are always
words.

specific ally

i love your forests.
let me see your trees.
we are subhuman
until
we engage the details
with emotional get-it cards.
maxed-out regrets
& unpaid debts
too soon forget
that our invisible hands are forced.

everything happens for a reason
that history has forged.

it's the way we rationalize action
& caramel frappuccinos
& faith in the shamans of the subconscious.

analyze the stories you tell yourself
take a census of your inner bards.
match pitch with their voices.
accept their perfections
& avoid their seditious stares.
embrace traditions,
the weight of practice.
use the word "i"
in new dimensions.

& when it becomes too much,
clutch
for
what?
what?

what?

cyberjava

there is poetry in agendas or friendships,
the mild utopia
of coffee or orgasms--

hopes and dreams
hopped up on
heliotrope yearnings
for fusion among worlds,

celebrations among tactile
configurations,

and the obvious difference
between clipping one's toenails
and giving oneself a pedicure.

hollywood is overrun by
headhunters and unicorns.

hearts are too.

the last silent reminders
of the wild--
palm trees & seagulls--
organize
for the final battle
& arrange themselves in columns
against the micro-managed.

the other side
cries out within,

as if something is missing in us,
erased by the
technogogues &
one-sided messiahs...

fine weather we've been having.

where do you want to do lunch?

i hear there are careers in nanotech.

in & out

topics circulate at parties
like instructions among ants,
viral ideas
of a collective unconscious.

backchannel antennae
of peripheral consciousness
register faint traces of
extra-prefrontal memes
vaguely overheard, overfelt, or overseen,
sublimated as
serendipity's spread,

an almost-erased bible of palimpsest
signs of the times
awaiting opportunities
to pounce
into relief.

being is acting
& acting is reacting,
the precise
& sacred geometry
of reflection,
deflection,
interjection,
& introspection.

eye contact isn't magic.
social mirrors either.
what feels immediate is always mediated.

& actually
(if we can believe the headlines)
the only initial difference
is between
in & out.

infinity

i knew
when we spoke
that our topics & tones
were defining us
in
negative space. there
we were, two
blobs,
indivisible
bumping up against a
universe of love
to be detected…

& the sumptuous flesh in
front of your teeth
was my morsel—
and i was a thigh
against your thigh
when you told me why we
may never be defined.

we may never be.

but until we swim
in the flood of our nevers,
let's champion each other's
presence where
the exclusions of our contact
will always share
what
only
makes us
one.

with bukowski's *cooperation*

bukowski sits at a window
& watches young girls' asses
which are attached to young girls.

i do too
& i also like tits.

connoisseurs,
bukowski & i.

we should start a club:
Men Who Obsess Over Supple Flesh.

membership would be exclusive.

imagine that!
"bukowski…attached to young girls!"
…by the cock
& otherwise
enjoying
tits & asses which are
ironically attached
to young girls which are
ironically attached
to beautiful sunny days
& an ocean of existence.

beethoven wrote symphonies about these
tunnel visions attached to tunnels of love with their
recipes for existence attached to recipes for consciousness of
young girls' asses attached to young girls.

americana

a squirrel runs
across the grey shingleroof
of the green woodpanel house
that isn't a house.

it's the kind of non-house in which
emily dickenson might have
secluded herself
to write poems about dying soldiers
she never met.

i mean,
it looks like a house
on what looks like a quaint little
neighborhood street,
but turn the corner
and the tell-tale signs
of being on a hollywood studio lot
kick in.

i once had an encounter with a woman
that was like that,
squirrel and all.
what she gave to my imagination
thrilled me.
"love!"
i thought.

just don't
turn the corner.

tact & subtext

like fiction & optimism,
tact & subtext
linger their marvelous bellyflops
& bellydances
on your lips.

without saying it,
in your best Sigmund Freud accent,
you ask subterranean questions like,
so, tell me about your childhood.

"are you from here?"

i'm drunk on the beer
of your segues.
is this foreplay?
& do you have the shovels
for some amethyst
fragment
of sacred text carved
in an ancient tongue,
long-lost & waiting
to be unearthed?

"oh really, where are you from?"

none of us is
from here.

drunk

as if german beer
that you eventually
feel
in the fingertips
of your ownmost being
were irrelevant to your
ownmost thinking,

or

as if
feeling the manifold
modes of consciousness
deconstruct the beauty of existence
to analyze the
prize
as practical,
you could do anything
but

laugh.

you know

the
always-waking.

rocks,
flesh,
sunshine
sometimes
give
up:
different-being.

surprise

surprise
is the element in
which we swim as
novelty is the soul of
growth tangerines
juice the sun of your
childhood to
KEEP UP!
as consciousness grows hair
only to
fuck the police
of social normativity with
HA!
that dances
to bass-guitar souls that
flow incoherently
into estuaries
of peacock-party-realities
that soothe over
bait-and-switch of
fundamental gravities.
it is
so human
to float.

zarathustra's serpent

"let me re-format your hard-drive!"
is an intimate request
soft-spoken,
& not too often accepted
wholesale.

if you believe that
beauty inheres the mundane,
openness to suggestion
is for those who are
wise as doves
& innocent as serpents
offering you food
for wisdom
& sustenance.

socrates knew how
to let knowers know
what they didn't know,
but the smooth-tongued snake
instead
created gods & goddesses
of apes.

good & evil:
before?
beyond?

these are
two approaches to
("what do you know?") &
("who told you?")
in
what do you want?

let me submit

being is passive.

the desire to be
is
the desire to be
adored
respected
loved.

being links.

being is being-of.

being been

you say,
"i am a dancer!"

but i, like dance itself,
say
"i, dance, am become by you!"

i am been by you.

you say,
"being is."

(because you secretly want to say,
"my being is.")

you want to say
"i am."

but i, like being itself,
do not say, "being is."
i do not say, "i am."

i say,
"i am become by you."

i am been by you.

workshop

it's not fair to ask me
to do something
that's not mine,

to put on boots that don't fit,
to tell my lovers i hate them,
or to send away the ocean.

there is a greatness
waiting to be mine.

i've heard the trees
whispering about it,
just before they handed me
the axe.

eye contact

the diving women
didn't duck
as they had
on other occasions,
so underwater
cupid's missiles
darted
& struck!

as above
cats sat by
to violin concertos,
so below
the waters
were concerned
with their blood
& maneuvers
& the weight
was adequate to task;

acceptance swam
with trust
till surface
business
interrupted with its shimmer.

the feminine toweled off as such
& bade *adieu*.

as if a kiss were too much
of a fuck.

iii.

venice beach experiment

dealer

it's not in the cards.
it's not in the stars.
causality
is distributed
elsewhere.

but this guy
keeps on saying,
"give me 5
cards!
any
cards!"

he asks like a junkie
asks for a fix.

"what do you think about more,
relationships or money?"
he says.

he mumbles, "neptune."

then,

"you're a communicator."

he tells me
i should play
the hand i'm dealt.

dreamvibe

hollywood
is full
of children
building forts
with wood & nails & paint

as the romp of humanity
keeps
heaving & thrusting
its cash across counters
its ocean of bodies
working
to sustain this
play.

here
if anywhere
vision is reality

if
vision is clear
then tongues will sing
& voices will be heard
& everything that floats
across the path
will become
diamond

meditation

to those who want to know
too much
too soon,
who dive into a fold
in the brain,
rushing headlong
toward details & divisions,
narrowing toward a singularity of oblivion—

read the history of philosophy
as a grimoire,
a primitive practice
of breath over neurons,
a meditation.

privilege your philosophical axons.
build cities of knowledge
in fields of memory.

& as you serve humanity,
pace yourself.

voyeurs & players

an amazing relationship
inhabits
                                        attention
                    between
        libido
            &
                      mise en scène.

it's not just that all else
becomes
                    invisible,

but also,
     what is visible
takes on a certain
                        exciting feel.

       "voyeurs" traffic
       in front-end pleasures—
               the commerce of the eye.

"players" traffic
in back-end pleasures—
       (hiding their voyeur-excitements,
       deferring them until consummation,
       waiting for their prize…)

               is there some unknown
                    excluded middle here?

some chemical
between the ink
      & the evening?

shepherds & midwives

flock-mentalities
proliferate
until
shepherds are struck
from books
from dialogues
from communities
where facilitating each other
is the rule.

fields of
acceptance
watered by rains
of enabling.

it's not about being right,
being smart, or
being in touch with truth, with
a capital t.

midwifery is serious business.

it's about joining in
the labor at hand,
ensuring that life is healthy,
that joy becomes complete,
& that the future remains
secure.

you

what counts as serendipity?

simultaneity?
succession?

what counts as confirmation?

does it mean you're on
a healthy path?

that you're right?

right?

as if motifs
floated through
the music of the spheres
for your benefit alone.

when you feel those
cosmic eyes
telescoped on you,
relax.

it's not your number.

keep dancing, always
to newer drums
& let your feet
consider
what it takes
to help the young.

do you?

it will have been
nice to meet you

again

in some
email-appropriate followup
world.

& here is the mystique:
you may be the one.

how does that feel?

we just met.

now silence is our only form
of communication.

a breath,
a relaxation,
& here I am

again.

everyone wants to connect.

do you?

ride

deconstruct your sexuality
along the lines
of your will to reality.

where is she going?

a shoestring
or
a seagull,
purse to purse.

resurrect
the weapons of desire
until
nothing is left
except
what's going on.

tantalus never reached the fruit.

don't be him.

jump.

& if the relics
of your monsters
scare
your bedspreads,

breathe.

letting go

should you
be recognized for beauty
or wisdom?

whose lands are these?

what crops grow here?

if, at any given time,
your character is the average of your
five closest friends,
what kinds of sobriety,
what pleasures,
inhere your wrestling
highest goals?

something slips.

fear of loss.

why fixate on the unlikely goal,
unless it is your life?

if starving,
why not
feed off others' praise?

why not be all that you can *seem* to be?

why
know yourself
when you can
display yourself?

or else
hypnotize yourself
into

letting go.

flow

the king
is just another
swimmer in the stream,

even if he is a philosopher
or a poet,
a privileged tangle
of focus & desire
that gets to say
what's next
for the body
politic.

this king,
this strongest habit,
naked,
bathing,
where peasants' perceptions
& merchants' machinations
undirt
& surface
to be received
again
into the grand dance.

king after king,
body after body,
silt, salmon, & starlight
are guests of this same
river.

identity

read dictionaries
read people

most of them are
tired & worn out,
spineless,
distressed,
over-psychoanalyzed
& very
self-absorbed—

sitting there
waiting
to be turned inside-out,
waiting
for some magic combination
to unlock
an inner transformation.

read up on dictionaries
read up on people

most of them have
entries for sentience
waiting to engage
waiting to be used in sentences
waiting to turn toward you
waiting for action and allegiance
as they flail
their kamikaze limbs
on a collision course with some
inner singularity
like a blackhole
of death.

what books assume

religion is chemically-titrated mania;
an intuition of order beyond the ordinary;
science fiction begging to become science fact;

orphaned Being clamoring for adoption;
possibility seeking incarnation;
the non-profit side of what you're doing;
or, as they say, "god's plan on man's business model."

the positive or negative evaluation
of our past behavior
& our possibilities for action
are where
perception is reality.

perception as reality
is where
religion,
root-metaphors,
double-entendres,
& "what you think is going on"
occur.

the sun peeks out
from behind the clouds
of
nursery rhymes
spells
& whatever else
we use
to train
the child inside.

training day

your imaginary friend
or that character you created
with the funny voice
to entertain your schoolmates

help

alleviate social anxiety
but fall far short
of that sticky stuff
that unifies your agendas
at any given time
& by which minds
are made & unmade.

untrained canines
endanger themselves
in worlds where trashcans
are full of broken glass.

they cannot ask questions
of master
traditions.

training is fear.

& when you can't say
"i can"
when you're broken
all you hear
are muffled mermaids
in your
inner ear.

anti-postmodernism

eschew the
convenient complexifications
of postmodern indexicalizations
when you could just say
"i."

by the same token,
destroy naïveté.

do you
live between
simple & complex
actions,
conversations,
& values?

then

tune in
to what's
called for.

lullaby

the prince slept soundly
under the responsibility of his birth
& the starlight of what was expected—

nobly bred,
nobly fed,

bloodlines want &
bloodhounds hunt
ally-laden
flocks & fields—

he grows to expect certain things of himself.

education,
manners,
courtship,
clothing,
valor,
vows
&
honor…

the queen suckles these
into her infant's bedtime
lullaby.

delivery

laugh out loud
at the phantasmagoria of life --
bodies
heaving, thrusting
drinking, clinking glasses,
raising cigarettes to mouths,
saluting,
respiring, sitting still,
conscripting themselves to the armies
of the appropriate.

love is the opposite of should

just as
tactical maneuvers
win battles
not lovers.

nostalgia is the opposite of life

& your existence is a joke
the universe tells
itself.

make it
hilarious.

heroes

desert moons
accumulate their small exceptions,
&
       slide

by degrees into suns.

do not praise them for their valor.

they laugh their matter
as they devour
vast spans of dark variables,

waiting for nothing,
especially not themselves,

to sing their oldest strings

       or hunt
       or fuck

into oblivion.

on praise & blame

you ask your snakes
to bite into the future.

you praise them when they do.

but when they turn &
bite your hand instead,

you assume they're blaming you.

assembly

our hearts & minds collaborate to dream

just as

the call of the future
    is traced
to some impressionistic mental picture
& the coordinates of its
familiar feeling—

truth is whatever we trust.

distinction

at any given time
you should never
have your entire life
planned out.

but at any given time
you should always
have your entire life
hoped out.

universal atheism

everyone's an atheist.

everyone believes
at least one god doesn't exist.

it's usually someone else's.

style

the most important thing
you can be in touch with is
your personal *style*—

how else would you
be able to say
when i'm cramping
it?

lovedrug

loving you
is a bit of madness,
the craziest idea i've ever had --

head over heels,
lovesick
on you,
lovedrug.

you're my future,
my fate,
my reason to exist.

even now,
my horses are kicking down
their doors,
frantic to run through your fields.

how to learn a name

the first few times
we spoke
i had trouble
remembering your name.

i usually use
some mnemonic device,
but i couldn't find one for you
that stuck.

then you captured my soul.

now that my being
has orbited your star
(which has no name)

your name
leaps to my lips
like a young deer,

as naturally
as
every breath
i take.

love

love
(and all idealism
for that matter)

is simply
a high note
in a symphony

which makes sense
only
amid rhythms
& harmonies

& everything that's come before --
(all motifs
of life & history)

and when it does...

amoeba

we amoebae --
constantly conforming
to containers
shape-shifting boundaries
of hopes & dreams
& social systems
(real or imagined)—

we are the motors of history
engulfing whatever
we find edible
& squirting ourselves
into it,
on it:

a question of diet
& environment.

& we imagine ourselves
connoisseurs,
even on contours
not bounded by walls
or objects—

our own weight
& desire
& fear
& gelatinous cytoplasm
keeps us

in.

(overheard in the subtext)

|i'd rather|
 |express|
   |my|
|sexuality|
 |in ways|
|that are less|
  |constricting|

houseguests

if i were to invoke
pablo neruda
at times like these
as the sun sets over the malibu mountains
& the hubbub of smiling patrons
ripples through *dunkelweiss*—

if i were to invoke
absent peter
or his mythical keys
to kingdoms beyond
or what it feels like
to mingle at university parties
among scholastics
who come & go
talking of
t.s. eliot
instead of
judas priest—

if i were to read
symbols into seagulls
or popes into palmtrees
or love into life
or the wealth of all my experience
into this world
that is happening now—

i would be doing the oldest injustice.
i would be doing the only thing i know how.

race

race
to the edge of the world
outside of time-frames
& rewards.

it's a game.

we all began
as sperm and egg,
and passed through infancy
to childhood.

the child in each of us
remembers:
we don't need reasons
to play.

counterpoint

reveal yourself. don't hide behind a mask.
your life's too short for this frivolity.
your answers sit and wait for me to ask.
your soul is guarded by your policy.

your policy is never to seem wrong.
appearances of impropriety
are devil's tri-tones banished from your song,
your conversation's outward piety.

the logic of your pleasure and your pain
are still betrayed by every tone & glance.
the inner workings of your cherished aims
unveil their steps inside this social dance.

the music of your happiness & woes
constrained by this: you won't step on my toes.

ucla

where neo-classical mammoths,
rivaled only by redwoods, house

minds
that have read
forests of books &

societies of scholars with
bellum omnes contra omnes
on their succulent
undersexed lips,

knowledge begins.

it grows
or is built
here
in this *sine qua non*,
this academic community,

where termites feel
buttressed by mounds of
traditions
& ideals,
by everything
they've
read
&
want...

but what would they do
without:

each other?

...or

...or
there is some old poetry
that resonates with this place—

some forgotten logic
of childhood environs
seduces you
to taste
old wine in new.

you wouldn't have
expected this
(or
maybe you would --)

this world,
this unity
that draws you
in.

lovespell

i've lived too well to weep a martyr's tears,
or wonder how i'll be interpreted,
or suckle compliments, or let my ears
hear lullabies in your superlatives.

our steady eye-contact is sleight-of-hand—
hypnosis veiling more than it reveals.
your *love* & *mystery* are shifting sands,
the superstitions of your chemicals.

you know i'm not an ego to be stroked
until its insecurities get off,
and yet you act as if you'd seen a ghost
you can't manipulate with gain or loss.

and though i love you more than words can tell,
i'm still immune to all your magic spells.

everything nothing

compare your lifetime to eternity.
how small and insignificant are you?
compare your years to moments as they fly.
how infinite are all the things you do?

and how discrete and singular is life--
the things you choose, the projects you delay?
divide your time by work, by kids, by wife
to calculate the science of your day.

beneath such atoms? particles & specks.
beneath the specks? more specks (if we could see).
our ever-keener instruments detect
no bottom to this archaeology.

where even zero is divisible:
the groups compose the individual.

leveling

the motives
you feel
may have been doubted
compound
into a mountain of justifications
for a million imagined
scenarios,
when if
you had relaxed
into my silence,
you would have seen forever
in my eyes.

now
the hills of your fear
must be
leveled.

venice beach experiment

the philosopher,
moonlighting as an actor,
sits here
drinking dunkelweiss &
smoking american spirits.

gregarious,
even in frivolous encounters,
he has the air of one
who has probably had
many women.

warm & open,
penetrating eyes,
still capable of reflection
& promise.

how does he
move so seamlessly
between conversations about
surfing
& books on
psychology & nihilism?

context

if the way you tip-toed
toward my sentiments
made you say it
differently,
embrace the difference.

it came from your lips

like a wild thing,
newly evolved
for fittest survival
in my environment.

& you were there, too,
fitting its sinews together,
creating
with the joy
of dionysus.

take your words
with you
as you leave
the home of my presence.

find a home for them.

fling them out
to a thousand galaxies
& see what
they return
with.

pain

your life depends upon the status quo,
invested in its expectation-sets.
communication is for those who know—
establishments are undermined by sex.

"the literal will make the world go round!"
"the cat is on the mat!" (or so they say).
where clarity forgets to be profound,
unsung pervasive power-networks play.

your will-to-honesty forgets its art—
your firm resistance slays your playful sport.
you lose the whole, controlling all the parts—
your unity, dissected into sorts.

and in your heart's desire to be plain,
you only link to others through your pain.

metamorphosis

layer by layer
peel back
the onion of the obvious
until there is
no longer onion
no brothers or sisters
fathers or mothers
goals or desires
pasts or futures
heres or theres
no specks of scientific matter
no principles
no reduction
nor anything to reduce
no explanation
no expectation
no meaning
& no should-for-meaning

no should

& thus—
no grief or joy

no shell
no core
no less
no more

a new math

atop the *yes-no* universe
sits a *yes-and* universe,
      a *yes-with-a-twist* universe

where *no*
& *not*
& *only*
& *limits*
don't exist as operators.

this is a new math
known to psychologists, hypnotists,
salespersons,
entrepreneurs,
& visionaries of attention
& focus
& hope
who know that

topics trump truth;
wants, worlds…

…& that what will be
is stronger
than
what is.

waterfront

every day here
primal creatures
in altered states
forsake
their scattered conversations
& erupt
in joyous applause
as the sun sets
behind the mountains—
as if to say,
"thank you."

every day.

this is
pure & true
religion.

intrusion

the capture is by no means incidental,
the machine of attention.

what you see
is
what you want.

what they think
is
what you should.

life has always been

clothing optional,
clothing functional,
clothing advertising

solidarity & schemes
for where you're going.

wondering if
you're accepted
or not
is so frivolous

& ubiquitous

until awareness
intrudes.

spectator sport

observing is the opposite
of participating.

some are good
at one
or the other...
...a few at both.

eyes follow desire;
posture & heads
what someone's into,
where they're going.

being & time

"be yourself"
doesn't mean,
"be who you've always been."

it means,
"be who you want to be."

meditation

ease your way
into the zone.

there is wisdom
in the calm.

then
look before you leap.

listen.

speak.

ode to my lover

sometime soon
you'll discover
a corner of my secret,
some second language
we both had forgotten
we speak.

then,
you'll achieve me without effort.
you'll sing to me
from your nest
somewhere above your ears,
and your song will ask
the only question
i know
how to answer.

observation

try
to not be hypnotized
by this comment...

(...or what is more,
by this *observation*)—

                      unfulfilled intentions
                            register
                        as tensions
                        in the body.

thisbe's eyelids

love itself
becomes dull
to protect the soul,
an iris occluded
by its own skin.

she waits
for her excitement
from the otherroom.

and when it comes,
she reads her own enigmas
between
the lines of force.

this is her food,
her pleasure.

she sends all of her powers
through these walls.

the turmoil of their architecture
does not deter.

flowers bloom
from the mortar
whose stones
weep amethyst tears.

dropping to the ground,
she awaits her lover's
return.

ode to an atheist with a god-complex

fire
writes off people
who have wills.

stars explode.

at the fringes,
planets are born,
populating voids
in peace.

rocks love sun,
lava.

there is a logic
to this,
a thin crust,
a fragile tune.

cells & oceans,
ferns & dinosaurs
live here.

clouds drip rain.

& you,
beloved—
the flowers of your beauty
are already finding their
bees.

mindstretch

serendipitous subtleties
spread their logic of
"look! this has happened before!"
while girls in white dresses
pray at altars.

magic is in the air,
the noticing of similarities.

synesthesias,
    symmetries,
        syncopations, &
           symphonies
sound.

"why?"
is a question we don't ask.

suggestion rules here,
"like to like"…

…here, where
synchrony is just
a stretching of the mind.

ask

let me be uninterpreted
like a scab
on a mimosa tree
no one ever bothers
to look at.

let me be in love
like disneyland
where rainbows flash
in lovers' eyes.

let me be of service
to everyone i meet
like a host
at a great banquet
of whom nothing
is too much to
ask.

what's with you?

what's with you?

you,
with your bicycle
locked to your memory,
cellphone locked
to your intelligence.

where did all these locks come from?

nothing can be left to chance,
or the magic of surprise.

buffalo,
    beetles,
        & especially squirrels
have their places, too.

trees need birds;
lilies, bees.

but these are locked
in a different struggle,
the same struggle.

they clutch life differently.

and you?

where is your watch?
   ...your wallet?
      ...your keys?

where did all these locks come from?

what's with you?

on bukowski & hollywood

male lesbians
& movie producers
have a special place
in their shorts for you.

amateurs pawn themselves
as professionals,
as curious little dogs
sniff, pee, & poop.

you've spun it your way already.

everyone has.

tao

the inexhaustible
subtlety of presence
pervades
&
inundates
what we are after,
wave after wave.

stumble through reality.

there is no other way.

ancient wisdom

use
what is going on
around you
to help you
slow down.

only then
does ancient wisdom
make its entry.

only then
will the hand of life
write in your
calligraphy.

on personal gods & household idols

the mouth
is where the cave
    & the tribe
       & the market

   collide—

the feeling of where fate is made
in a two-step with desire.

nothing translates this sunrise,
   this personal painting
everyone sees.

portrait of a young woman as an artist

her parents had a pool,
  a jacuzzi,
palm trees,
  & an orange tree.

they were presbyterian.

her mind carried its survival knife
  of words & pictures
& information
  about sexualized bodies
  & media feminism.

she enjoyed confronting the obvious
  in others
and this time
  it was obvious
that a pair of heels
had been left
  on a lace tablecloth
beside the pool.

worlds apart

philosophizing is nothing
without humanizing.

but how does one humanize
the lizard's desire for the fly?

this is not a point-and-click operation.

some enlightenment,
budding in obscure gardens
of *le siècle des lumières*
hardly deters
the shit-grabbing
circus-monkeys.

"lit crit
has its hemisphere
in which to safely
convalesce,"

kant mumbles
to the other inmates,
one of whom is wearing
pablo neruda's hat.

meanwhile,
in hollywood,
five producers are meeting at seven
at the bourgeois pig
to discuss rumi.

on families & self-resemblance

the only way to get outside yourself
is to compare.

build a mirror of archimedean logics.

point new fingers.

reorganize.

don't be afraid to ask
    whatever-is-not-you
for its logic,
its love.

a new drumbeat.

whatever.

be curious.

become unfamiliar.

here

fantasy is a marvelous thing.
you go places in your head.
whatever *i* flies there
returns transformed.
dreamscapes alter landscapes.
the *where* & the *why*
often elude you—
and even the *who*
is doing it...
...but something is different now,
now that you have found *me*,
my love,
here
in this wondrous place.

for vanessa

he was teaching her tactics
   in the subtext
when i walked in with a pipe full of smoke
& said, "is this a joke?"

"don't you know?" he said, "we're talking
   about revolution!"
i said,
   "so why are you whispering?"

heartcry

brilliance doesn't excuse
condescension,
nor discrimination, violence.

greatness is what we need—
the capacity to listen, learn,
& be generous.

dismissing others' observations
by insulting their word-choice
forgets what words are.

so how do we begin to speak?

it would be nice to make
the groupwill
our individual wills.

but where will we swear
solidarity, allegiance
to the flags of our deepest expectations?

what wars will we fight
& what will our banners look
like?

...to the beat

everything everywhere
   within the range
of your perception
   or imagination
is a possible soundtrack
   for your
      experience.

two people, one evening

i made out
last night
with a hollywood script-writer
over a bottle of scotch.

i was drinking.

she already had.

she said i made her head spin,
which must have been
something for her head—
full as it was of
magic, tarot, astrology, jesus.

she sat on my lap
and squeezed a kiss out of me,
told me i was ego,
told me i was her first
lover to be invited in.

she told me she was very private
and that we wouldn't be having sex.

i told her it was my considered opinion that she should articulate
her id and lose some weight.

rhapsody on rilke

once
there was something i loved,
the same kind of thing
lost when rome fell.

once
cobblestones reassured
the wary moon.

now,
as i sit & think of you,
as the thousand hands
 of expectation
hold me still,
i wonder—

is waking worth it?

didn't we both prefer
the dream?

this is a good avocado

the F.D.A. didn't approve
the fruit i bought
from the old latino street vendor.

the F.D.A. didn't approve
   or disapprove
the transaction.

this avocado,
   those coins—
don't exist.

they are questions
from another answer.

no F.D.A., no F.B.I., no D.E.A.,
no controls.

the only safety in place
was the old man's smile,
his reassurances of quality,
his grandchildren playing in the background,
his humanity.

this is an ancient exchange.

guide

it was about
the power she gave
through her breach
of trust—

a birth,
painful for me,
a new need
to take responsibility,
power.

"why?"
isn't the question.

she wasn't in her right mind.

it became time,
through the pain,
to guide.

for a.r.w.

i could've spent the time that i enjoyed
with suitors far more suitable than you.
my head alone is getting me annoyed—
my gut-reactions know what they would do.

my heart is left between them to decide,
& when my lips are pressed against your breast,
or when my eyes are lost inside your eyes,
my heart believes it's found a place to rest.

but when you exit and forget yourself,
& seek adventure with your company,
& lose discrimination's subtle help,
forgetting all the things you've known in me,

my heart remembers that my head is right—
& blinding love becomes reminding sight.

for you

she re-established
her sexual power
by choking him.

they were
his cigarettes,
of course.

she rolled her eyes,
rolled over in bed,
wanted his hands on her.

…those 45 minutes
seemed like eternity
holding her
in bed.

eyes, hearts & tongues

"...
'crime is nothing
    but a spot
     of not
knowing where to lay
  your head.

and where's the fault
  in that?'

asked the fox
  to the hen."

the clever wolf smiled
& sat back
as he finished the story
& looked around
into the eyes
of his pack.

metaphor

how it sinks in
    &
how it sticks
  to that sticky place
that makes us do
  what we do
    is
what's important.

we need noses
  to complement
    our new eyes.

this is beyond analysis
  but not beyond feeling
    for one
      sweet
      succulent
        taste.

billy idol

his hands
were in
everyone's vagina
because he loved
what he had to do.

he slept at her place,
almost without asking,
made eggs in the morning,
and left.

he cut off his sleeves
without a second thought.

booze was not his devil.
at times, his muse.

he wanted what he wanted.

he left
something for the eggs.

fame

down
sunset
to pch
to zuma
one meets
the ghosts of old hollywood,
spirits of old-guard dreams,
old wealth
put to new tasks—
praying to i-phones,
remembering burningman,
bursting at the seams
with the elation-torment of humanity—
well-manicured souls
of erstwhile great apes,
forgetting their anger & fear
as they step into their temples of
beauty.

not black & white

the brooding,
complex character-type
rarely
attracts roles
but
often attracts
women.

why?

is it because
women like
mystery?
   challenge?
      nurturing?

the actor
   behind the type,
behind his disguises for emotion,
laughs.

autopoesis

yesterday i had a drive;
today i had another—
from mansions to the wilderness,
my will went undercover.

while

yesterday i had a dream,
today's was much more lucid—
the body must be fed & weaned
of privilege & abuses.

ode to anaxagoras & deleuze

the wilderness
isn't just something
that can be willed
earnestly
out of existence.
what colony, hive, pack, troupe,
or brood
could do this?

life comes in all sizes,
from one cell
to billions.
but all is life.
cooperation is the glue,
the organization.
& how did that machine
evolve?

most angels are too busy
dancing
on their pins & needles
to hear
the mind
in
things.

given

the best love
isn't blind
idealism
but deliberate
hope
for futures full
of dopamine-rush
responsibility.

conscious love,
considerate of
generations & corruptions,
giving itself over
to wild ecstasy.

this is our love,
beloved.

let's build our homes
in each other
and in the work
our hands have been
given.

playgrounds

is your body
  a political map
or
  a geographical map?

both at once?
neither?

what distinctions
& lines
& circles
does it make?

when?

suppose
  you're drinking beer
& i put my hand
on your crotch.

what then?

does this have anything to do with playgrounds?

select company

three or four
  degrees
of separation
  can be
too close for
  comfort.

who
  you bring
within your valence
  can either
bring
  fear
    or
plenty.

    choose wisely.

we depend
  on others'
    commerce.

i'm familiar
  with this place.
i've been here
    before.

index of opening lines

first line	page
a hidden word inside my heart and head	98
a squirrel runs across the grey shingleroof	120
alluring & adept	99
am i a victim? am i a slave?	6
amid the chaos of routinely	68
an amazing relationship inhabits attention	133
as if german beer	122
at any given time	149
atop the yes-no universe	169
be yourself	173
being is passive	125
brilliance doesn't excuse condescension	191
bukowski sits at a window	119
compare your lifetime to eternity.	163
crime is nothing but a spot of not knowing where to lay your head.	199
curious upright beast	107
dare to think	92
death is not a razor	105
death is passive	114
deconstruct your sexuality	137
desert moons accumulate their small exceptions	146
down sunset to pch	202
dream, oyster	103
ease your way into the zone	174
eschew the convenient complexifications	143
especially at times like these	111
even though no one told you where to close the parentheses	59
every day here, primal creatures in altered states	170
everyone's an atheist	150
everything everywhere	192
fantasy is a marvelous thing.	189
fire writes off people who have wills	178

first line	**page**
flock-mentalities proliferate	134
for us life is like name-brand candy	78
give me something before you go	112
he was teaching her tactics in the subtext	190
her parents had a pool, a jacuzzi, palm trees, & an orange tree.	186
his hands were in everyone's vagina	201
hollywood is full of children	131
how do definitions finitize?	52
how it sinks in & how it sticks	200
i am the first omnisexual	20
i bring perfection to the grid.	82
i could've spent the time that i enjoyed	197
i have almost made a companion of the feral cat	69
i knew when we spoke that our topics and tones were defining us	118
i love your forests. let me see your trees.	115
i made out last night with a hollywood script-writer	193
i said everything that i wanted to say	67
i sat by rosa parks in economy class	75
i sent a mentality in your direction	87
i want you to take something beautiful from me	96
i write in your presence & a flock of insecurities take flight	86
i'd rather express my sexuality	156
if I were to invoke pablo neruda	157
if the way you tiptoed toward my sentiments	166
i'm not expecting profound revelations	84
in a graveyard that defies gravity	70
in all of your beauty, your approach is like lightning	56
in the moonlight, the cardboard cylinder	73
in this war we're the spies	43
is it too much to ask for your facts not your politics	106
is your body a political map or a geographical map?	207
it was about the power she gave	196
it will have been nice to meet you	136
it's all about you babe	77

first line	page
it's espionage & under the sheets is just a hiding place.	100
it's not fair to ask me to do something that's not mine	127
it's not in the cards	130
i've lived too well to weep a martyr's tears	162
karma lingers from the skating rink	29
laugh out loud at the phantasmagoria of life	145
layer by layer peel back the onion of the obvious	168
let me be uninterpreted like a scab	180
let me reformat your hard-drive	124
LIBERTY. statue of. statute love	8
libidinal labels are libel	58
like fiction & optimism	121
lit, like a cigarette	3
love (and all idealism, for that matter)	154
love is a one-hour trip to the louvre	102
love itself becomes dull	177
loving you is a bit of madness	152
male lesbians & movie producers	182
medusa's in the mirror, starstruck	55
not a day goes by that I don't make a million little choices	63
observing is the opposite of participating	172
once there was something i loved,	194
one can never BE enough for one's parents.	79
open your eyes. what do you see?	45
or maybe it was something about the newness of the situation	89
or there is some old poetry	161
our hearts & minds collaborate to dream	148
oatmeal stout slides down the gullet	110
persuasion is vibration	83
philosophizing is nothing without humanizing.	187
race to the edge of the world	158
read dictionaries. read people.	140
religion is chemically-titrated mania	141
rest sleepers for these are not my primary buttocks	81

first line	page
reveal yourself. don't hide behind a mask.	159
roll out the red carpet	108
serendipitous subtleties spread their logic	179
she re-established her sexual power by choking him.	198
should you be recognized for beauty or wisdom?	138
shut the fuck up and listen	17
sometime soon you'll discover a corner of my secret	175
somniloquent visions of hiphop blogospheres	53
strum through the manual	109
summon your sorrows, dressed in pajamas	76
surprise is the element in which we swim	123
the best love is not blind idealism	206
the brooding, complex character-type	203
the brown mass, with its earthy aroma	26
the capture is by no means accidental	171
the circle of eager humans, clubs in hand	42
the death of possessions	85
the diving women didn't duck	128
the earth shits diamonds	113
the F.D.A. didn't approve the fruit i bought	195
the first few times we spoke	153
the inexhaustible subtlety of presence	183
the king is just another swimmer in the stream	139
the most important thing in poetry is honesty	94
the most important thing you can be in touch with	151
the motives you feel	164
the mouth is where the cave & the tribe & the market collide.	185
the only way to get outside yourself is to compare.	188
the paths of thought that run	32
the prince slept soundly	144
the rarified air of theory	101
the silence deafens	50
the time of year for christmas cheer	40
the velvet distance of spectacular vaginas	72

first line	page
the wilderness isn't just something that can be willed	205
there is poetry in agendas or friendships	116
this is a poem	95
this is my truth in action.	47
this philosopher, moonlighting as an actor	165
those who want to know too much, too soon	132
three or four degrees of separation	208
topics circulate at parties	117
truth is like weather.	91
try not to be hypnotized	176
two nodes diverged in a neural knot	71
under the weather is an understatement	104
use what is going on around you to help you slow down.	184
we amoebae -- constantly conforming	155
we mutants walk among you	35
what counts as serendipity?	135
what do you mean to advertise, mango?	25
what is the price of sleep?	12
what not to ask is not a kitten	74
what's with you?	181
whatever people see & hear	61
where neo-classical mammoths	160
wormholes & blackholes congregate.	65
yesterday i had a drive;	204
you ask your snakes to bite into the future	147
you have seen me in all of my humanity	31
you say, "I am a dancer!"	126
your imaginary friend	142
your life depends upon the status quo,	167
your pimp is a pimple, tootsie.	88
your soul walks naked in your eyes	93
you're lucky, yellow town	30

www.ingramcontent.com/pod-product-compliance
Lightning Source LLC
Chambersburg PA
CBHW071452040426
42444CB00008B/1310